KEVIN'S JOURNEY

Casey Clark

Dedicated to my two sons,

Kevin & Brian

For without them, I would be nothing.

Kevin, myself and Brian.

Author's Note

Kevin was a happy little boy until the day he was diagnosed with ALL Leukemia at the young age of 3.

The whole family was thrown into a tailspin involving hospital visits, chemotherapy and an amount of radiation that the government later banned because it was too much for the brain, especially in a child. This was a three-year protocol.

At the age of 5, Kevin was diagnosed with testicular cancer which left him sterile and for the rest of his life, he would need testosterone shots, or he would mentally and physically revert to 16 years of age.

Kevin relapsed with ALL Leukemia when he was 7 years old having just stopped the chemotherapy months prior.

Brain cells are the only cells in our body that do not replicate. Kevin's radiation left him with huge craters in his brain, which forced him to learn everything in an alternative manner. His maturity level is at 20 years of age.

The medical team told me that he would never be able to live on his own, be able to drive, count money or hold down a job. I never bought into that theory and continued to work and drive him to the best of his ability.

After finishing his treatments, he completed high school with his class. By this time, he held down a job and was able to drive and ventured out to his own apartment.

Slowly, in time, things were not adding up. Kevin had become addicted to drugs just to fit in with his younger peers. One morning, I discovered Kevin downstairs in our house, in a drug-induced coma. At the hospital, the doctors kept him in a coma for a week to rid his body of the toxins-then into an inhouse treatment center.

Kevin eventually married, which after 10 years ended in divorce because his wife had been mentally abusing him for years.

Kevin will be 48 years old in 2024. He lives on his own, has a very good job at a children's hospital and is appreciating his life day by day.

I am so proud of my son, Kevin.

Casey Clark

Foreword

My name is Kevin.

This book is about my life until today.

It's raw, truthful, serious and funny.

My life.

A life that was never destined to go past 5 years of age. As I am writing this, I am 48 years old.

Mom has tried to be as honest and truthful in telling my story.

I hope that someone reading this book will never give up on the people you love, no matter how hard their journey is.

1.

"We need something to save our marriage," I proclaimed to Steve, hoping that he would respond. It would have been a miracle if he did. If it weren't on TV, then a response would not be given. Steve would come home from work during the week, eat dinner and then watch TV until bedtime. On the weekends, he would eat breakfast and then watch TV all day. There was no communication or interaction with me or our young son, Brian.

"Did you hear me?" I asked in frustration.

"Yeah, I did, what do you want?" Steve answered without taking his eyes off the TV.

I took his response as an open door.

"I was thinking that having a baby would work, maybe save our marriage," I said gently.

Steve and I had been married for 6 years. Every year that passed, I became more aware of how little we had in common. The main difference was that he was an introvert, and I was everyone's friend. We had no friends in common in our lives that we could share experiences or just simply be social with. He never wanted to do things or go places with other people or even with just each other.

Steve and I were high school sweethearts which turned into a young marriage and a child being born 10 months later. Our son, Brian, was 5 years old when I approached Steve with the idea of having another child.

When a commercial came on, I figured that my asking for another child would elicit a yes or no response. Nothing. I decided to take matters into my own hands and turned off the TV.

Steve's head came up with a snap. "What the hell did you just do?" he yelled.

Finally. "Do you want to have another baby?" I yelled back at him.

"No," Steve positively said.

"Why not? Brian is 5 years old and in school, and we can do without my salary for a few months," I argued.

"No," again was Steve's response.

I thought about it for just a minute and then decided to go off my birth control pills. It was a risky move, but I looked at it as a last-ditch effort to save my marriage with Steve.

About a year ago, I had forgotten to take my birth control pills more than a few times. One morning, I woke up bleeding. I ran to the bathroom and felt something drop into the toilet. When I examined it, I was scared. It was a sac about one inch long. I called my doctor, but he was out of town, so I spoke with the doctor on call. He told me that I most likely experienced a miscarriage and to take it easy for a few days; in addition, I would experience some spotting for about four days. Losing a baby was just the worst experience I had to contend with, and I had to do it alone. Steve was unaware of me going off the birth control pills.

The next day, Steve asked me why I was so depressed lately. All I could do was just shrug my shoulders and walk away.

2.

'Wow, I think I'm pregnant,' I thought six months after taking my last birth control pill. This was a time before home pregnancy tests were available. I had to go to my OBGYN for confirmation. There was an old saying for this confirmation. If you were indeed pregnant, the doctor would say, "The rabbit died." I never understood that saying. The doctor would have you urinate in a cup and what…the rabbit would drink it?

After my doctor examined me, he asked that I get dressed and meet him in his office. Nervously, I put my clothes on, making sure that all the buttons were in the correct spot, grabbed my purse, and headed down the hallway.

"Have a seat, Karen," Dr. Roberts said. I sat on the very edge of the chair as I listened to the doctor begin to explain, in detail, why he hadn't wanted me to get pregnant.

"Given the fact that you have had an extreme case of endometriosis in the past, it is likely that you will not carry this baby full term. I am estimating that five months will be the most. I'm sorry, but one of the reasons that I put you on birth control pills is so that pregnancy would be prevented," Dr. Roberts said in a very firm voice.

"I know, but I really wanted a baby. I'm just about finished with my three months of nausea, and I will faithfully take my prenatal vitamins that you prescribe," I said firmly.

"Well, just be prepared to either carry the baby the entire full term and deliver a stillborn baby or have some issues and we will have to prematurely deliver it by C-section," Dr. Roberts said while looking at me sternly but spoke with a caring voice.

Now I had to go home and tell Steve the good/bad news. I was not looking forward to an 'I told you so' response.

All the way home, I kept thinking of different ways to tell him, finally deciding on a 'just rip off the bandage' method. I pulled the car into the driveway and let out a sigh of relief. Steve's car was not there, which meant that I had a few minutes to gather my thoughts. I went in, changed clothes, and waited for Steve to come home from work. Brian would be at school for another hour. Just then, I heard Steve's car with the familiar door slam following.

"Hey," Steve said.

"Hey back. Can we sit down and talk for a minute before Brian gets home from school?" I asked. Steve sat down and stared at me.

"I went to the doctor today, and he said that I was pregnant," I blurted out.

Steve leaned forward and thought about what I had said. He got up from the couch and put his arms around me. "Well, another mouth to feed, I guess."

I had never felt so loved.

3.

My pregnancy was monitored very closely by my doctor and his staff. I did everything I was told and crossed my fingers. Steve was even helping around the house. Brian was curious and I answered his questions the best that I could. When the baby started to move, if Brian was around, I let him feel the movement. His eyes got so big with wonder. Four and then five months passed without any signs of trouble.

I worked as an accounting manager for a large St. Louis firm up until my seventh month of pregnancy, very careful to take all precautions. At the beginning of my eighth month, I went to work with a blizzard looming and approaching fast. The meteorologists were going crazy, updating every half hour. After lunch, I finally asked my boss if I could leave at two. Looking out the window, it appeared to have snowed eight or more inches and the snowplows were working as best as they could but not keeping up.

Steve, Brian, and I lived in a mobile home community about 30 miles away from the St. Louis city limits. I called Steve before I left work and told him that I was on my way home. The commute normally takes 20 minutes. He told me the weather was so bad that he had called into work to say that he wasn't coming in. Steve never missed work.

"Okay then, just letting you know that I'm leaving," I said as I hung up. I never heard him say, 'be careful.'

So off I went, very slowly, my pregnant belly trying to steer for me. Cars were sliding and some were even in ditches. I realized that I was shaking with fear. At the entrance to our community, my car started to swerve. There was nothing I could do and into a ditch I went. This was the great era before cell phones. So, I turned off my car and sat there and just cried.

Suddenly, a man was knocking on my window asking if I was okay.

Through my tears, I said that I was okay, but I was also eight months pregnant. He asked me if I could open the door. Wiping my tears and grabbing my keys, I was able to pry the door open enough, with his help, to get out. He hugged me gently, put his arm around me and guided me toward his warm, awaiting car. He turned up the heat full blast to keep me warm. I told him where I lived, and he headed that way.

When we got to my mobile home, he jumped out of the car, opened my door, and helped me up the steps. No sooner did that happen than Steve opened the door to our mobile home.

"What the hell?" he asked, surprised.

Before I could answer, the nice man said, "Dude, her car went off into a ditch at the entrance of the mobile home park. I happened to be behind her and was able to help her out of the car and bring her here."

Steve then told me to get inside and change into dry clothes. He thanked the guy and closed the door.

"Now I will have to pay for a tow truck, and hopefully, you have not done any damage to the car," Steve yelled at me.

I went into the bedroom to change and just cried into the pillow from our bed. I was still shaking, but the baby didn't seem to notice that anything had happened.

When I came out of the bedroom, I just glared at Steve and went back to lay down, holding my swollen belly protecting the baby. Steve was in the living room and continued watching whatever had held him captive until I'd gotten home.

4.

As true to form with Brian, this baby broke my water in bed, always a rude awakening. It was 4:00 am, and the plan was to drop Brian off at Steve's sister's house and go to the hospital. As I was getting dressed and putting things together, Steve came into the bedroom to tell me it was snowing and we already had several inches of snow on the ground. We threw everything in the car, buckled Brian in, and off we went.

It was a slow go, but we were moving, and my contractions were getting closer. As we approached Steve's sister's house, we had forgotten that she lived at the bottom of a hill. Being that it was the middle of March, we didn't think that snow would be a problem. We phoned ahead to let her know we were coming.

Going down the hill wasn't too much of a problem, but after dropping Brian off, the uphill climb was a chore. I said every prayer that I could think of. The baby must have sensed my fear because it started kicking like crazy, wanting to come out. "Hold on, little dude," I said.

We finally made it up the hill and headed toward the hospital. As I mentioned before, this was before cell phones, as well as pregnancy tests and sonograms, to tell parents the sex of the baby beforehand if they wanted to know.

Steve and I both wanted a girl the first time we had Brian, so we were really hoping this pregnancy would result in a girl. I wasn't in labor nearly as long as I had been with Brian. With Brian, my water broke on Wednesday, but he hadn't come into the world until Saturday.

In the delivery room, the nurse happily informed me that I had a healthy baby boy. I had arranged with my doctor to have sleeping gas during the delivery, so no more pain after some contractions. When I woke up, the nurse was wiping my head, then she showed my baby to me and said, "Congratulations, you have a healthy baby boy," and I said, "I went through all this trouble for a baby that looks just like the one I have at home!"

I woke up after what seemed like hours to my pediatrician telling me that she was in the nursery and I had a beautiful, healthy baby girl.

"No," I told her. "It is a boy."

The pediatrician told me that she had a few more moms to see, but after that, she would swing by the nursery and do double-check.

"No, please check right now," I demanded. I must have sounded powerful because she left my room in a hurry. It was hard to doze off or think of anything else until she came back.

Suddenly, my pediatrician waltzed into my room. "You are right, you do have a baby boy. Congratulations."

5.

Life in our household was normal for the first few years as a family of four. I was working full-time and attending college at night to obtain my marketing/management degree. Brian was in school, Kevin was in daycare, and Steve was working in the factory where he had worked since leaving the army. Steve would come right home from work, grab a snack and watch TV. It was my responsibility to pick up Kevin from daycare and Brian from the sitter's. If it was a school night for me, I also had to make sure Steve and the boys had dinner before I left.

When Kevin was around 2 ½ years old, I noticed that the skin on his legs appeared red and blotchy. I took him to the doctor, and upon examining him, the doctor said that he was allergic to green household plants. When we got home, I quickly threw out all the plants, regardless of their color, that we had in the house. I had never heard of that before, but he was a doctor, and I was not.

Kevin started to get better, or so I thought. A month later, he developed large blisters on his legs. He cried and told me that they hurt. I took him to a different doctor, who, after examining him, said that it was an allergic reaction to something, but he didn't know what. The doctor began a series of tests on Kevin over several weeks, but no matter what test he administered, none came back positive. Again, he was a doctor, and I was not.

One afternoon, Kevin's daycare called me at work. His teacher said, "Kevin's blisters have burst, and they are bleeding. He is saying that he can't walk. We think you should take him to the emergency room."

My heart just sank. What could be wrong with him? He was just a small boy. Steve met us in the ER at the hospital close to our home. Steve had to carry him everywhere, because Kevin just couldn't walk. After 30 minutes, we headed into an exam room. Kevin was frightened. All he could do was hang on to me and cry. The wailing Kevin was doing from our exam room probably made the doctor come in a little sooner.

The doctor took Kevin's medical history, which was very little up until a few months ago. As Kevin cried louder, I became more frustrated. He examined his legs and told us to take him downtown to Cardinal Glennon Hospital for Children in St. Louis.

Steve carried Kevin to the car and laid him in the back seat, and we sped toward the children's hospital. By the time we got there, it was 9:00 pm, and all three of us were tired. Luckily, my mom picked up Brian from school, and he stayed with my parents for the night. Mom would take Brian to school in the morning, then she would go to work.

Again, a doctor came into the exam room and took Kevin's medical history, but this time they did a blood test (CBC). Kevin was exhausted by then and almost out of tears. I told him when the doctor came back and said we could go home, we would all go to sleep, and tomorrow we would take him to McDonald's, his favorite place in the whole world. To make time pass, I invented every kind of story I could think of to take his mind off the current situation.

After about an hour, the exam room door opened slowly, and the doctor came in. "Kevin's white blood cells and red blood cells are all out of whack. Something is wrong. We are going to keep him overnight and make him comfortable. Tomorrow, we are going to do a spinal tap to get the answers we need. I'm sorry it is not the news that you wanted to hear," the doctor said and looked at us with sympathy.

We had to wait about two hours before Kevin was admitted and put into a room. Kevin had to have a private room because he most likely had an infection. When we got up to his room, it was painted with all sorts of balloons and animals. I put him into the hospital pajamas, laid him down in bed and rubbed his back until he fell asleep. Then I sat down in the recliner and just cried. I guess I fell asleep at some point.

Since Kevin had to spend the night, Steve left after he heard this because he had to go to work the next day. I also had a job that required me to come in every day, but Kevin needed me, and I was not going to let him down.

6.

The next morning, I encouraged Kevin to eat a little breakfast. The nurse said they would probably give Kevin his spinal tap around noon.

"What's a spinal tap, mom?" Kevin asked me.

I took a deep breath and was honest with him so he could be somewhat prepared. I needed coffee badly, so I told Kevin I would be right back and went to the cafeteria for some coffee and a muffin to take back up to his room.

Being a Friday, I called Steve at work to let him know what was happening and when the spinal tap would probably be.

"I have to play in my soccer league tonight, so I won't be able to come to the hospital, but I will leave

Brian with your parents, and you can pick him up there," Steve informed me.

Poor Brian. I felt like for the last 24 hours, I had neglected him. My parents adored both boys, being their only grandchildren, and they tended to dote on and spoil them.

I called my sister, Judy, who is six years younger than me, to see if she would come to stay with us. She attended St. Louis University, but I knew she had no classes on Fridays.

"I'm on my way," Judy said. When she arrived, the doctor was explaining that Kevin would be partially sedated because if you moved at all during a spinal tap, you could be paralyzed. The doctor asked me

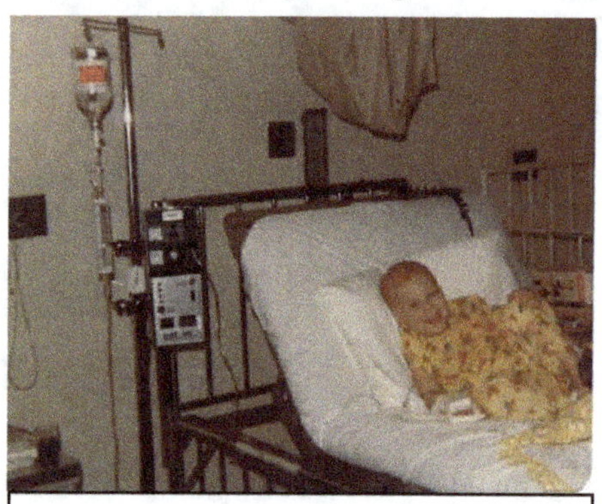

Kevin's first hospital stay

if I could be there to calm him down if needed. "Yes, of course I will." And off we went. The room was stark white and looked like a surgical room. Very different from the rest of the hospital and its rooms.

They asked me to put Kevin into a fetal position so his back was stretched and exposed. I sat down so I was facing his head. I calmly sang our favorite song and whispered loving words to him. He was such a trooper and never moved.

Afterwards, Kevin was wheeled back to his room while I followed, where Judy was waiting. He had fallen asleep and looked like my perfect angel. About two hours later, the doctors came into the room and asked me if my husband was there. I told them no.

"We need to have a meeting with you and your husband to discuss Kevin's results," one doctor said.

"Well, my husband will not be back until tomorrow, so let's go," I said affirmatively. Judy stayed with Kevin, moving closer to hold his hand.

We entered a small meeting room. Already seated was another doctor and a nun. Doctor Connor introduced me to Doctor Chun and Sister Anne. Doctor Connor explained that Doctor Chun would also be treating Kevin. Sister Anne was there to take notes.

I started thinking—wait a minute, he had just had a spinal tap, and we can just go home, right?

Doctor Connor explained that the spinal tap revealed that Kevin had ALL leukemia. If treated rigorously, he would have a somewhat fighting chance to survive.

Leukemia begins in the bone marrow; it may spread to the central nervous system, the brain, and spinal cord. A key element is whether the cells look mature or immature. The most immature cells are called blasts. Having too many blasts in the spinal fluid is a typical sign of leukemia.

After meeting with the doctors, a nurse pulled me aside and said that there was a support group of parents for children with cancer called The Candlelighter Society, and they had a meeting scheduled for that night at 7:00 pm downstairs in one of the meeting rooms. She offered to come back to the hospital after her shift to attend the meeting with us. I accepted her offer. I called Steve and told him of Kevin's test results and that he needed to come back to the hospital as soon as possible. His soccer was not important right then, Kevin was. Our lives have been forever changed and he needed to be there with Kevin and me.

Patty, the oncology nurse, met Steve and me in Kevin's room a little before 7:00 pm. Together we rode the elevator downstairs to the meeting room. My heart was in my stomach, not knowing what to expect, plus leaving Kevin alone in his room. I put a movie into the VCR just below the TV. I told him we would be back just as the movie ended and if he needed anything, to hit the nurse button on the remote control. He held the control in his little hands with a strong grip.

The meeting room was filled with parents when we arrived. Everyone seemed to know Nurse Patty as she introduced us. They started with a few minutes from last month's meeting, plus upcoming events to raise money for The Candlelighter Society, which helped children fight cancer and raised money for general funding.

Neither Steve nor I had been to any support group of any kind and we both felt like a fish out of water. The moderator opened the floor to whomever would like to speak, ask questions, or share stories. Many people took advantage of this, allowing us to learn so much more about the different cancers these families were dealing with. It was mind-boggling. I happened to glance at the clock and discovered that we had been there for 90 minutes. I whispered to Steve that we had to leave to get back to Kevin. He readily agreed. As we entered Kevin's room, we found the movie over, and he was fast asleep. It sure was one long day for all of us.

7.

The doctors wanted to start Kevin on a regimen ASAP. This would entail chemotherapy every day for three years and strong radiation—1500 rads to his brain once a month for six months. The radiation was just in case the leukemia cells were hiding there, and blood tests during the chemo were to help discover any damage to the liver, kidneys, or other organs. MRIs were not widely used until 1977.

I told them to do whatever they needed to do. Looking down at Kevin while he was sleeping, I just couldn't imagine this little boy having so much wrong with him. His first round of chemo would be done in the hospital to see how he handled it and to allow the nurses and doctors to monitor his condition.

Monday would be Kevin's first round of chemotherapy. I told Steve to bring me a change of clothes for two days and he and Brian could come for a visit. Brian was only eight and it would be his first time in a hospital, outside of a short visit to have his tonsils out. We all needed to wear surgical masks when being around Kevin—less chance of an infection.

Monday morning seemed to come early as the nurses began to prep Kevin for his first round of chemo. I told him that they were going to put a needle in his arm and that's how he was going to get the medicine that would make him feel better. When I explained the procedure to Kevin, I always was very honest with him. The needle went in, and the tears began, both Kevin and mine. Watching the poison go into his body was hard, just hoping that they did the trick. He was also given three medications orally that he would have to take daily for many years.

Steve and Brian arrived around noon. I could see the fear in Brian's eyes when he saw his little brother being hooked up to different liquid bags hanging above his head. Earlier that morning, I went down to the gift shop to get Brian a book and a puzzle and Kevin a stuffed monkey. Kevin grabbed the monkey and held it close to his heart. "Your name is Monk-Monk," Kevin said to the monkey.

After about 3 hours, the bags were empty, and the needle was taken out of Kevin's arm. He was very tired and finally went to sleep. Steve and Brian went home so Brain could get some sleep as well. I tried to make Brian every bit of a priority as Kevin. However, I couldn't be in two places at once. Kevin's pale, little body lying against the white sheets was about all that I could handle.

Later that night, Kevin woke up crying and began throwing up. I rang the nurse and said that Kevin was sick and needed a change of pajamas. The nurse gave Kevin some medicine via another needle in his veins to help with the nausea. That seemed to help.

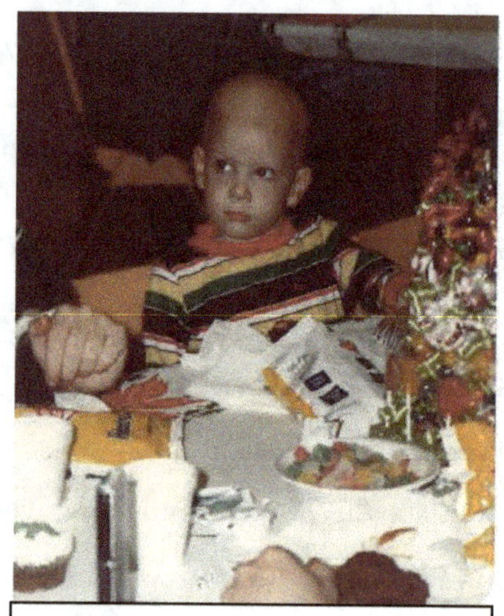

Candlelighter's Christmas

party

By this time, most of the veins in Kevin's arms had collapsed due to over-tapping, so they decided the next best place to put a new IV was in his upper foot, with half of a plastic cup around it. They asked me to leave the room, as it was going to be very painful, and they were going to have to hold Kevin down. As I was walking down the hall, I could hear him screaming 'Mommy'. I just couldn't take it anymore—I closed my eyes and just crumbled to the floor.

Kevin's body received the chemo well, so we finally got to go home. I filled his three different prescriptions, and we settled down to a new norm. Once a week, Kevin went to the hospital to have his blood drawn and checked for abnormalities. We usually went on Fridays.

8.

I have used the pronoun "I" quite a bit because Steve was either at work, playing soccer or just with the guys.

I know I must have been exhausted, but I told Steve that I didn't need three kids and wanted a divorce. He seemed to be surprised and told me that I could not do this without him. "Watch me," I said.

It was hard, but I had my family's support. They lived nearby and were able to help take Brian to and from school. Our lives revolved around Kevin and his needs. Brian came with us for Kevin's treatments so he could understand and be patient. Steve never called to offer to take Kevin to his treatments or just come with us.

Kevin went to preschool as often as he could to maintain some sort of normalcy. One day, at school, he broke his arm. I picked him up from preschool and headed to the hospital, where they put a cast on it. What a sight—a little boy with no hair and his arm in a cast.

During one of his hospital stays, he was hooked up to several IVs attached to a poll. I left for a little bit to get something to eat. When I came back, Kevin had gone across the room with his IV pole, arm in a cast and a bottle of soapy bubbles under his neck. Where there's a will, there's a way.

After a series of blood tests that week, I noticed that the finger they had pierced had turned black. I quickly called the doctor, who told me to take him to the ER. Luckily, he just had an infection and we added penicillin to the daily regimen.

Kevin's real personality comes out!

After about two weeks of oral chemotherapy, Kevin started vomiting. That wracked his entire little body. When I was holding on to his head, I noticed his hair was falling out. This site was very hard for me to bear. My baby was being tortured.

What do you do with a head of curly red hair?

It was hard for Kevin to swallow pills. While I was at the pharmacy, I noticed a cup with a lid slit into it that you would put your pills in. It was black. This was during the Star Wars days. I told Kevin that it was his Darth Vader cup. It worked. One check in the positive column.

The doctors told me of another concern. If Kevin ever had any contact with a person with measles, he was to be brought directly into the ER. With his chemo, the measles could quickly kill him. He was not allowed to receive any childhood immunizations because it would interfere with his chemo. I had to obtain several signatures from doctors to this effect so he could be allowed in school.

So, of course, about two weeks back at preschool, the teacher called and said that a mother had just notified her that her little girl had a bad case of measles. A letter had been sent to each child's home that attended the school to the effect that Kevin was not to be near anyone with measles. As soon as I finished the short conversation with the teacher, I picked Kevin up from school and took him directly to the hospital. They had to admit him so that they could monitor his progress. He had to be given platelets from a pregnant woman to combat the measles. This sounded so bizarre, but it worked and in just two days we were back home.

9.

For the next three years, Kevin would take his oral medication daily, have his blood tested weekly, and receive a spinal tap every three months.

After we finished the first month, Kevin was ready for his first of many radiation treatments. He was again admitted to the hospital for his first radiation and then outpatient thereafter. A doctor came in and marked up Kevin's face with a magic marker where the radiation would be centered on. I always tried to make games out of these things to lessen the seriousness of the treatments. The nurse came and took him away. I was told to stay in the room and Kevin would be back in an hour. The first of six treatments. What to do while I waited for my little boy to come back from having his brain radiated? Finally, the door opened, and he was wheeled back into the room. I didn't think his skin could get any whiter.

When Kevin was not in the hospital, he returned to daycare. My employer was very understanding with the amount of time I had to take off. Brian also needed my attention, and I gave him what he needed the best I could. By the divorce decree, Steve was supposed to take the boys every other weekend, which would also allow me to work extra hours and get caught up on my schoolwork. Usually, however, he only took them once a month.

It was during this time that I started to date Ron, a CPA from work. He was divorced and had a teenage son. The boys loved him, and he got along with them as well. But I was not ready to get remarried. Between a full-time job, going to school, and being a single mother to two boys, one of whom was very ill.

As if I didn't have enough on my plate, I felt like I needed to give back in some way. I decided to throw myself into The Candlelighters Society. This group of brave parents had so much to share with me. I volunteered to be the editor of a brand-new product that I was introducing: The CandleLighter, a newsletter. This was right up my alley and I enjoyed it very much. Each month, I would compose it, take it to the printer, and mail it to each family, though it turned out to be more of a booklet than a newsletter. It was about seven pages and 8 ½ by 11 inches folded in half.

Kevin is playing "doctor" with his brother Brian.

I would get feedback, plus articles from families, in addition to any input from the National Association.

I was the editor for about three years. During that time, I found something very interesting. The post office required that I bundle the newsletters by ZIP code. After the second month I had been bundling, I noticed that two distinct counties had an inordinate number of newsletters, St. Charles County and Jefferson County. Both counties border St. Louis. I dug deeper. I narrowed down the counties by streets. In both counties, the streets affected were very close to water treatment or abandoned weapons plants. In St. Charles County, the treatment plant was adjacent to an abandoned storage facility for World War II weapons. In Jefferson County, the ZIP code was next to a water treatment plant. Shaken with this knowledge, I contacted a local news station to see if they were interested in the data that I had collected. Not only were they interested, but they also sent a team of reporters to investigate. Two days later, their findings were broadcast during the evening news, though there was an immediate denial that anything was wrong despite my investigation.

The story eventually died a slow death. My only hope is that the families affected have since moved. When Kevin was born, we lived in Jefferson County until he was about two years old. Why Kevin was affected and not Brian, I don't know. What I do know is that I made it a point to drink as much water as possible while I was pregnant with Kevin. To this day, I've had breast cancer twice and too many skin cancers to count.

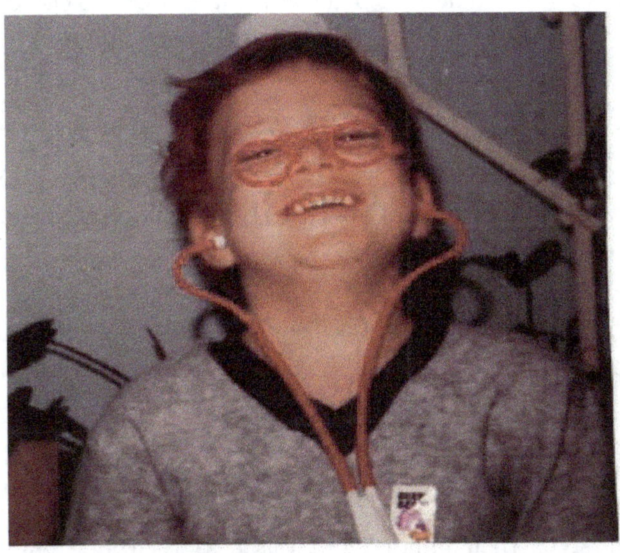

10.

Christmas time was coming, and we were all excited to help make Kevin's Christmas special. Ron, the boys, and I put up the tree and hung the ornaments, only breaking two. Then we had a contest to see who could pick up the most tinsel from the floor. Christmas morning came and did not disappoint either boy. Around 1:00 pm, it was time to go to Steve's side of the family. I decided to accompany the boys and Steve to his family's gathering, even though we were no longer together. Ron took the opportunity to visit his parents and his son.

We loaded up the car with gifts and were on our way. Steve's family wasn't large, but with a brother and sister plus their children, it was a good group. The magical time came when the presents were passed out to all the children. In the frenzy of it all, I noticed that Kevin opened two gifts—a small puzzle and a Matchbox car. Noticeably less than the other kids. I looked at Kevin and saw that he was busy looking around the tree for anything else with his name on it.

Everything under the tree had been opened and distributed. I'm not one for putting dollar figures on gifts, but looking around, I noticed that each child seemed to get well over $100.00 worth of gifts. The estimate of Kevin's gifts was maybe $20.00.

I looked at Steve and he just shrugged his shoulders. I decided to speak with his mom in private, presenting the fact that Kevin had received very little compared to the other kids. She shook her head and said, "We just figured he was going to die soon anyway, so why spend a bunch of money?"

11.

Kevin was now entering first grade. I met with the principal beforehand to inform her of his medical condition and that he would be missing quite a few days from school, plus the fact that he didn't have any hair. She suggested that he wear a baseball hat so that it wouldn't be so noticeable. It was a great idea, so I took Kevin to the store to pick out a hat. I thought maybe he would select a St. Louis Cardinals or Blues baseball-style hat.

OMG, after looking at several hats, he selected one in the far corner on the bottom shelf. It was a hat with a raccoon's head on the top….this was so Kevin! If he didn't mind wearing it, it was a done deal.

Kevin's first day of school.

The first morning, he got dressed and proudly put on his hat. Yes, he got stares, laughs, and fingers pointed at him, and even the older kids took the hat off and passed it to each other.

"Let's play keep away from this little kid!" they would shout.

One morning, the school nurse called me to come to meet with her as soon as possible. Dropping everything, I rushed to the school with many random thoughts racing through my head.

The nurse met me with a kind smile on her face. Apparently, Kevin went to his teacher and said, "My balls itch." Not wanting to see exactly what the problem was, she thought it would be best if I did. So, the nurse went to retrieve Kevin.

"Kevin, I understand that you told Mrs. Dunn that your balls itch, is that right?" I asked.

"Yes," he replied. I took him aside so I could look at what he was talking about in private. His testicles were indeed swollen beyond belief. Right then and there, I called his doctor, who told me to bring him to the clinic. So off we went on the familiar route we drove so often.

In the exam room, the doctor looked at Kevin and decided he needed a CAT scan of the area. Waiting and worrying was something I was doing a lot lately. The nurse brought Kevin back to the room and said that the doctor would be in shortly. I sat him on my lap and hugged him until he squirmed. Within a few minutes, the doctor did indeed return without his normal assuring smile.

"Kevin has testicular cancer, and we should treat it as soon as possible; also, we found that he has a hernia in the area as well," Dr. Chun stated.

Wow, I thought, will this ever end? The doctor said that Kevin would need radiation in the affected area. The radiation would take care of the cancer in his testicles. They also needed to operate for the hernia. The doctor also informed me that due to the radiation to his testicles, this will render him sterile and not be able to have children. The radiation would take place every Friday around 2:00 pm for six weeks.

We scheduled the hernia surgery for a week from Tuesday as an outpatient procedure, so at least he got to come home. The radiation would begin the next day.

He had just finished his cranial radiation. He was receiving 1500 rads once a month, in case the leukemia was hiding in his brain. One month after he finished the radiation, the government said that the high dosage he received was not necessary based on the fact that the leukemia might only be hiding there.

The waiting week for surgery was long, but it finally came, and into the hospital we went. They repaired the hernia, and it was minimally invasive.

12.

I had been dating Ron, who I had met in my office, for about two years. He had an adult son, so I was initially worried about him being a father to my two young children. Getting remarried was not a problem with Steve, as he got married three months after our divorce became final. Ron loved the boys, especially Brian, and I loved having a partner again to share the good and the bad with. Ron and I were married at the beginning of our 3rd year of dating.

By the time Kevin was 7 years old, he had finished his chemotherapy and radiation for leukemia, as well as the radiation on his testicles. We decided to celebrate by taking the boys to Disney World in Orlando,

Florida. The morning that we were going to leave, I woke up Kevin with a picture of Mickey Mouse.

"Do you want to go to see Mickey today?" I anxiously asked him. His eyes lit up and he jumped out of bed; we were already packed and ready to go. Off we went for a much-needed vacation. The boys were inseparable, with not a care in the world.

When we returned, Kevin was in 2nd grade. He was doing well, but I noticed that he was getting tired easily and having a difficult time concentrating. On our next clinic visit, they drew blood to make sure everything was going according to plan. After an hour, the doctor came into our room and looked at Kevin sleeping in my arms.

"Kevin has relapsed with leukemia," he said.

I just stared at him not knowing what to say.

"What does this mean?" I asked the doctor in disbelief.

"Two more years of chemotherapy with another drug added," Dr. Conner said.

"What about radiation?" I inquired, not ready for an answer.

"No, no radiation, unless we find that there is a reason to do so, but we think Kevin's leukemia is strictly in the blood, which is a good thing," he explained.

I thought to myself —a good thing would've been for him not to get sick in the first place.

Through the years, we have made friends with other children with cancer and their families, but I noticed that in the past year, I hadn't seen them, so I asked the doctor.

"In Kevin's age group, and with his protocol, out of 15 children, just Kevin and one other girl have survived. We are doing our best to continue this small achievement, but you asked, and I wanted to be honest with you," the doctor said softly.

13.

Okay, we are in for the fight of our lives. We did it once, we can do it again. Kevin's hair was starting to come back, and he would lose all of it again. I called his teacher and principal, informing them of what the doctor had told me. His teacher said the next day was picture day for his class.

"Well, if Kevin wants, he will be wearing his raccoon hat, that's just the way it will be," I explained.

His teacher agreed and added, "Some of the students do not understand what Kevin is going through and why he doesn't have any hair."

An idea came to me. "Would it be possible to have a very short assembly in the gym so that everyone hears the same thing at the same time?" I asked.

"I think that would be a great idea if you would explain everything to them about what is going on with Kevin," his teacher said.

"Not me, but Kevin, if he is willing to do so. I will be there for backup and further explanation, but if they heard it straight from the 'horse's mouth,' it would be better, and he could tell them in a childlike way."

In two days, the principal arranged an assembly, with Kevin and his medical ordeal being the subject matter. Kevin said that he would do it. Oh my gosh, here is this 2nd grader with the raccoon hat going on stage in front of the whole school to explain his medical situation. Of course, I was in attendance.

That morning, Kevin walked up on stage and stood there and looked around. At first, I didn't think he would say anything, but then he began.

"I have leukemia and that is why I wear a hat. I lost all my hair because I must take so many medicines every day. It hurts my feelings when you take my hat off and throw it around. I also hear you laughing at me…why?"

The teacher asked Kevin what leukemia was and how the doctors were treating it. I started to get up to explain, but then I heard Kevin.

"Well, I think my blood is very sick. I take eight pills a day in my Darth Vader cup. Every time I go into the clinic, they put a small needle into my fingers to get blood so they can look at it. Sometimes when I go, they put a long needle into my back and I must stay still because if I don't, I won't be able to move forever."

The teacher asked if there were any questions. One of the 5th graders raised his hand.

"Are you going to die?" he asked.

Kevin thought about this for a minute then answered, "Sure, we are all going to die someday."

Hardly a dry eye in the gym.

Kevin proudly throwing away his empty pill containers.

I noticed that Kevin was having a few balancing problems, so I enrolled him in dance classes. I know some of the football players dance to strengthen their leg muscles and improve agility. I used this fact to convince Kevin this was a good thing. In his class, for tap and ballet, there were 10 children—nine girls and Kevin. Guess who always got the good parts and center stage? Kevin, with his new red curly hair. My mom made his costumes for the recitals. He danced for one year—that's all I could get out of him—but I do think it helped.

Kevin in his ballet outfit.

Kevin and his tap dancing

outfit.

14.

On one of the hundreds of visits to the clinic, the doctor asked to speak with me privately. The nurse took Kevin to the playroom. My mind was racing about all the horrible things the doctor wanted to meet with me about.

Kevin showing missing teeth.

The doctor started off with, "We have new data to share with you about Kevin. When you radiate the brain, those cells that were affected die. The brain is the only thing in the body that does not replicate itself. Therefore, Kevin has many holes in his brain. At best, he will have to learn to compensate for his shortfalls. The studies shows that most likely, he will never learn to drive, count money, and he will be able to read, but will be unable to understand what he has just read and will never be able to hold down a job or live on his own."

I listened carefully, all the while shaking with each statement. I waited for the doctor to finish before saying, "So the high doses of radiation that you gave him many times over were just in case the leukemia was hiding in the brain—we never should have done this, correct?"

"Well, it was the best method we had at the time," the doctor explained.

I had noticed that Kevin was not learning as fast as the other kids, but I thought it was because he had missed so much school. I scheduled a meeting with his teacher and the principal for the next day.

Kevin and Brian, young brothers.

The principal told me that there is a state-funded program called 'Resource.' It finds a child's weakness in learning e.g., math, reading, etc., and during their regular time for learning these subjects, they will remove them from their class and go to a resource room, where a special education teacher will help them learn these subjects. The resource help will follow through college. This sounded great until they said that Kevin would not be eligible. He was not born this way or was not this way due to an accident. So, my child was a square peg trying to fit into a round hole.

I looked at both women, and very calmly said, "Kevin has a right to the best education possible and through no fault of his own had this happen to his brain. You will put him into the resource program, even if I must go to the Governor myself."

The principal and teacher looked at one another with wide eyes. Finally, the principal said, "Let me put together a program for Kevin and we can meet again."

15.

Kevin was 10 years old and had two separate rounds of chemo behind him. His hair was back and had to be cut every two months. He was in the resource program at school, which helped as best as it could. He was starting to realize that he was different in many ways. He always gravitated toward the 'underdog' and had a few friends that he could relate to.

Kevin and Brian, best friends.

I decided not to buy into the fact that he would never hold down a job, count money, learn to drive, or live on his own. I treated him the same way I treated Brian.

Summertime rolled around and I was working for a leading construction company. At 16 years old, Brian was highly intelligent. I got him a job in my office, filing and doing simple paperwork. The company also owned four apartment communities. Certain mornings, on my way to work, I dropped Kevin off at one of the communities to pull weeds and get a little extra money. At noon, I picked him up and brought him home to be a kid again. He only worked every other morning, but it gave him a sense of responsibility, plus a little spending money.

Every two months, Kevin went back to the hospital to have his blood drawn and tested. This was such a stressful time. If Brian didn't have school, he asked to go with us. The older he got, the more interested he became.

In 1989, I graduated college on a Friday and opened a new business with my friend on Monday. We specialized in marketing, graphic design, and advertising to business-to-business customers. I had money saved up when I left the construction company and used that for seed money. The business was successful and really didn't take up any more of my time than the office job did.

When Brian turned 17, one of the oncologists treating Kevin asked if Brian would like to work in his lab two days a week after school and during the Summer. Brian was over the moon with this information; he didn't care if he never got paid. I was so very proud of him. I tried to divide my time equally between the boys, but if Brian felt otherwise, he never mentioned it.

Brian got accepted to Baylor University in Waco, Texas. He had a scholarship with the University of Missouri, where all his other friends went. "Mom, I can't go there because there would be too much partying," Brian clarified to me.

How proud could a mom be? However, Waco was up to 10 hours drive from St. Louis. Again, this was a time before cell phones and personal laptop computers were for instant communication.

When the time came for me to take Brian to Baylor, I dropped Kevin off at my mom's. I wanted the experience to be just for Brian and myself.

Baylor was a beautiful university. Brian's roommate had not arrived yet. I left him to wander around campus while I went to a 'Welcoming Parents' luncheon. One thing they said was a must was to not have any communication with your student for the first week. By the end of the first week, both the parents and students would be somewhat adjusted. The only phone Brian had was a wall phone at the end of his floor in his dorm for everyone to use. When the time came for me to leave, I looked in my rear-view mirror, to see Brian standing on the sidewalk, waving. I cried from Waco to St. Louis. Before we left home, I closed Brian's bedroom door. I just couldn't stand to see it empty.

My mom dropped Kevin off, and we talked about the past weekend. Suddenly, we heard Kevin crying. He had opened Brian's door. "I miss my brother!" The door was never closed after that.

16.

While Brian was away from school, I noticed our family dynamic was changing. Ron had always favored Brian over Kevin. How does one do that? Maybe he was jealous. Ron was very strict with Kevin and accepted a 'no laziness' attitude toward him. If I weren't home, Kevin would tell me that Ron had hit and pushed him while calling him lazy for not doing his chores perfectly. Ron was also beginning to be verbally abusive with me as well.

Ron and I were having difficulties in our marriage. I suspected that he was jealous of the relationship that he thought Kevin and I had. Even though I loved my sons equally, he never saw that. Through the years, he became meaner to Kevin and eventually emotionally abusive to me. Kevin and I were both suffering at the hands of this monster that I married. He held an important position at the construction company and had vast amounts of wealth, but all of that paled in comparison to the way Kevin and I were treated. With Brian away, he never saw any of this happening. I arranged for Kevin to begin to see a psychologist to deal with his feelings. After a few weeks, she asked to speak with me. We met while Kevin waited in the next room. She only said one sentence to me: "Get yourself and Kevin out of that house."

That was all the ammunition I needed to make the all-important decision to leave Ron and the terror behind. We rented a condo a few miles away and began a new life for both of us.

Brian graduated with honors four years later. One month after graduation, he got married in Waco, Texas. Kevin was 15 years old and included in the wedding. Yes, I cried through the entire ceremony. Right after Brian and his wife moved into an apartment in Waco, he got a call to attend the St. Louis University

School of Medicine. Wow, I had him back in St. Louis for at least four more years.

I met a man, Larry, and we had been dating for a while. Both boys liked him, which was a bonus for me. At 15, Kevin was itching to get his driver's permit. Herein lies the problem: with his learning disability, he couldn't pass the drivers' permit test which was in written form. Somehow, Larry was able to teach Kevin to pass his written test and his driving test.

I went to the Fall parents meeting at his school. I only had two teachers to meet with, one being his full-time teacher and his resource teacher, Ms. Franze. Ms. Franze knew how to get through to Kevin in a way no one else did. She taught him through middle school, then got permission to transfer to high school so she could help him graduate after four years. She was an angel in his pocket.

My sister, Judy and Kevin.

Not paying any attention to the doctors warning him about not being able to drive, hold down a job, count money, or live on his own, Kevin got a job at a fast-food restaurant, one he could walk to. He did not work at the cash register but followed directions that they laid out for him, and had his own spending money and savings account. This was big, another hurdle jumped through.

However, even bigger was the fact that Larry helped him pass his driver's test and even get his permit. Scared as I was, we began looking for a car. An old one made of metal for protection. Fortunately, we found one. Kevin drove back and forth between school and work. I didn't let him drive for pleasure for quite a while. Six months later, he passed his driver's

Kevin's first car.

test and was officially driving whenever he wanted.

I started to recognize that Kevin had developed a strange trend toward the people he was friends with. He usually had three or four guys that he was close with, then after about six months, he'd drop them and start with another group of friends. This behavior was very noticeable. He seemed to hang with groups of four or five guys in them, which he then recycled every six months to a year over and over. I asked him about this behavior, and he said in a matter-of-fact tone,

"I cannot get too close to anyone because if I do, they might die."

I had never realized that he had formed this way of thinking, back when he was going to the cancer clinic and he noticed that when he made friends with the other kids, the next thing he knew, they were dying.

When Kevin graduated from high school, it was a very special occasion. We had Ms. Franze sit with us and after it was over, Kevin gave her a large bouquet of flowers. Again, not a dry eye in the house.

Kevin's high school graduation.

17.

Kevin was getting tired of working in fast food. One of my clients and former neighbor when we lived with Ron, was president of a large corporation. His son and Kevin were the same age and often hung out together. I asked him if he had a job opening for Kevin.

Kevin and Brian ready for a

St. Louis Cardinal game

"What can he do?" he asked. After thinking for a minute, I said, "He can file, make copies, and general clerking duties." He did have an opening or created one.

So, Kevin dressed in his 'hang up' clothes and off to work he went. We drove him there once so he would know exactly where to go.

Three months later, Kevin wanted to rent an apartment. Larry and I found a one-bedroom apartment that was great for just him. It was hard to see him go and live on his own, but I knew it was for the best. He lived in his one-bedroom apartment for about a year. He knew a friend who wanted to rent with him. His lease was up on his one bedroom, so the timing was good. Wow, this was so big: being able to count money, drive, hold down a job, and now live on his own.

Healthwise, he had not had any more leukemia relapses, but did have skin cancer removed about every six months. He saw a doctor once a week to have his blood drawn to make sure he didn't have any abnormalities in his blood and to also get a testosterone shot. He was seeing an adult internist at the time. Kevin needed the shot to help him retain a level of maturity, e.g., facial hair, body hair, and some maturity. Without the shot, he would digress to being about 16 years of age, mentally and physically. The shots were because of testicular cancer and were very important.

We found a 2 bedroom, 2 bath apartment that he and his friend could afford and was in between our house and his work. He was so excited, but we were very worried, but trying not to show it.

I told him that he needed to cash his check, then come over and I would put the money in specified envelopes for his bills to help him learn to budget. He came over for Sunday dinner every week so we could catch up and do the budget.

Kevin began dating a girl named Marsha. She was still in high school, but there was only a two-year difference between them. They seemed to be getting along well and were always together. This was Kevin's first girlfriend. Larry spoke with Kevin about always wearing a condom. Although he was sterile because of testicular cancer, there were multiple diseases that he could get and who knew how his body would react to them.

One day, Kevin called me and said that Marsha had to go to Chicago with her older sister's husband to pick up a car that their aunt wanted them to have. Since Christy, Marsha's sister, worked, Marsha volunteered to go with him.

An overnight trip turned out to be three days. Upon returning, Marsha told Kevin that she wanted to break up with him due to the recent fact that she had fallen in love with her sister's husband who was married, had three children and was 10 years older than her. Good riddance, I thought as I coached Kevin on how to deal with this latest event in his life.

Fun at the pool, Kevin being Kevin.

Things were going well, his bills were being paid, he had a good job, and was living on his own. One Sunday, Kevin said he got an additional job working a few nights and weekends being a dishwasher at a local restaurant. So, not only did he have one job that the doctors said he would never have, but two. Two paychecks plus tips…wow. I told Kevin he could keep his tips for additional spending money. One Sunday, he let us know that his roommate moved out suddenly.

"Well, you better find another one pretty quickly," we said.

Larry and I discussed it and decided to invest in a condo and let Kevin rent from us rather than throwing away his money on renting from a stranger.

<h1 style="text-align:center">18.</h1>

Larry and I got married, with both boys' blessings, in Florida. Larry had never been married before or had any children, but the union was seamless regarding the boys. Kevin adored him and Larry made sure to let him know that he was his mother's husband, not his stepfather. He also told him that he would be his friend forever.

On a perfectly good Sunday afternoon, Kevin informed us that he quit his job at my client's company to work full-time instead of part-time at a local restaurant. He said that the owner would provide him with medical insurance plus work for 40 hours a week. Kevin said that the owner also said that he would be making more at his restaurant than at the company.

After telling us this, Kevin looked up at us with tears in his eyes and said,

"Some of the guys at the other job were making fun of me for not knowing things."

Yep, Mama bear came out! "Okay, but you still need to give me all of your money from your check so we can put it into the envelopes."

"I found another roommate already; he works at the restaurant with me," Kevin said.

Today was as good a day as ever to tell him my medical news. "Kevin, I have been diagnosed with breast cancer." Saying it out loud brought a level of realization to me. Kevin turned to look at me with a matter-of-fact glance and said, "It's okay mom, no big deal. I had cancer many times and look at me!"

I don't know what I expected, but that wasn't it.

Two handsome brothers, Brian and Kevin.

19.

Things were going along smoothly until the shit hit the fan. Larry and I had been out shopping and when we got home, I noticed a red light flashing on the answering machine.

Kevin's voice came through rather meekly saying, "Mom, I need to talk to you, it's important." What could be so important that it couldn't wait until Sunday dinner? I called him back, hearing Kevin cry on the other end as he sputtered out the statement, "Mom, I'm addicted to drugs, and I don't know what to do."

I didn't want to address this over the phone, so I told him we would discuss it in person the next day at Sunday dinner. Wow, all the thoughts that went through the back of my mind came forward. He had been coming up short on his cash to be put into the envelopes, but he said that people owed him money and he would get it back, only he didn't. He was losing weight and looked somewhat pale.

Sunday afternoon came, and I told him we would discuss it after dinner. I tried to prepare and make dinner as if everything was normal. After the dishes were cleared away, we sat back down.

"What do you mean, you are addicted to drugs?" I asked.

20.

With his head almost down to the table, Kevin confessed, "Well, I'm addicted to drugs."

He looked up and his eyes were red from crying.

"Explain yourself," I shot back.

"Well, the younger guys at work asked me if I wanted to smoke some weed, and I said yes because I didn't want to be the only one who was different. Then I tried cocaine. I liked the way it made me feel and I fit in with the guys. But now, I want it every day and I can't say 'no' to myself or the drugs," Kevin explained.

"How are you buying drugs and paying your bills?" I asked him.

"I am not paying any of my bills. I sort of just ignore them, and I use my tips for some additional drugs. The credit card companies keep calling me and I just hang up on them. I just got a notice that my condo payment is two months past due. Darren, my roommate, suddenly moved out," he said.

"How often are you doing this?" I asked.

"Every day," he cried…literally.

"So, you aren't paying your bills, you just said you lost another roommate maybe because you are doing drugs at home, and you've been lying to me," I said while calculating the damage.

Kevin nodded, his head still down as he continued to cry.

"Are you wanting to quit?" I asked him, hopeful.

"Yes, that's why I told you, " He said.

"All right, let me see everything that you are behind in, and I will get you caught up. I also want to see your paycheck stubs so I can see exactly how much you get paid. You will go back to putting cash in your envelopes every week," I explained. Kevin was so upset; I doubted that he heard a word that I had said.

Looking back, I see that this was a mistake. I should have never bailed him out or should never have trusted him with cash at hand. Kevin agreed to everything, and we hugged, and he left. Having never had to deal with this before, Larry and I were at a loss on how to deal with this.

21.

About one month later, around 6:00 pm, I got a phone call from Kevin that someone had broken into his condo and messed things up and stole his new big screen TV. I drove over as quickly as I could. When I entered the place, it was somewhat of a mess, and yes, the TV was not there.

Kevin showed me how the lock on the patio door was compromised and that is probably how they had gotten in. I looked around at the 'controlled mess' and said, "We need to call the police and make a report."

"Do we have to?" Kevin pleaded.

"Yes, we do," I replied. Something told me to go into the kitchen and look around; Kevin was right behind me asking what I was looking for. Under the sink, I found a smoke pipe used for inhaling cocaine. I picked it up and shoved it into Kevin's chest and told him to go out and throw it in the dumpster. I watched him to make sure that he did indeed do it.

The police showed up and took the report. He then took me aside and said that I might be careful about who Kevin was hanging around with. I understood completely.

When the police left, I told Kevin to completely clean up the mess that was in every room in the condo. Multiple pizza boxes, fast food wrappers, and uneaten food. His bed didn't have any sheets on it, just a big ball of covers. Clothes everywhere.

I told Kevin he was to come and live with us and we were putting the condo up for sale and selling all his furniture.

Obviously, he didn't like that suggestion, but what could he say? So, I had him pack up a few things for a day or two until we could permanently figure things out.

Larry and I discussed the situation in great length. We didn't know it at the time, but Kevin sold his TV in exchange for drugs. And the lies continue.

We moved Kevin into our guest room and decided that the condo was such a mess that it needed to be gutted and refurbished before we could put it on the market. Of course, that was up to Larry and me.

With the little savings Kevin had, we bought new appliances and paint. Every weekend, Larry and I were there painting and cleaning, while Kevin worked and picked up every shift he could. I went online and bought several drug testing kits. I told Kevin we were going to drug test him every two weeks.

22.

One night I looked at the clock and it was 2:00 am, well past the time Kevin should've been home. I got dressed and jumped in my car and went up to the restaurant/bar where he was working. At that hour of the morning, there were still several people standing outside smoking. I pulled up to them and rolled down the car window.

"Do any of you know where Kevin is?" I asked in the calmest voice that I had.

"I think he said he was going home," one girl offered. He was not at my home, which meant that he was at his condo. I had not taken his key away—bad mistake.

I arrived and sure enough, his car was parked outside, with no visible lights turned on inside. "Shit," I said to myself. I was so very tired of this mess. The only piece of furniture that was in there was a recliner, as well as a ladder. I knocked a few times, to no answer, so I used my key.

I entered the condo and Kevin was sitting in the recliner, high as a kite. I looked around and there was paint everywhere, including the areas that we had just painted. The walls in the condo looked like people had painted graffiti on them.

"Kevin!" I yelled. His eyes fluttered and he moaned. "What are you doing here, and what happened to the paint?" I asked.

He mumbled some more, so I got in his ear and yelled my question once more.

"I thought I would help you guys paint, then I got tired and fell asleep," he offered up as a viable solution to the obvious problem.

I looked around at the awful mess and then went into the kitchen. I noticed that one of his burners on the electric stove was turned on and there was a teaspoon by it.

I completely lost it. I took the spoon and confronted him with it.

"What is this?" I again yelled.

"Ah, a spoon," he whispered.

"And what did you use it for?" I asked, knowing full well he had cooked heroin with it. He got very defensive and said, "I don't know."

"That's it, get yourself up and get in the car. Give me your condo key," I commanded.

Kevin got up, put his shoes on, gave me the key, and followed me to my car, where he slept the whole short ride home. I kept thinking to myself, "What am I going to tell Larry?"

I was so very mad I couldn't see straight. When we got home, I told him to go into his room and go to sleep.

Larry was still asleep and was unaware of the unfortunate events that had taken place. I had to stay up for a while to calm down and think about what to do next, knowing full well that I had to get up in just three hours to get ready for work.

About 8:00 am, I called one of my coworkers to tell her I would be late coming to work. Larry left for work without me telling him what had gone on in the wee hours of the morning. There was no sense in both of us being late for work.

At 10:00am, I woke Kevin up and told him he needed to call into work to say that he would not be going in. He did as he was told. After that, I told him to sit down.

"I thought you were done with drugs?" I questioned him.

"I was for a while, but people kept offering it to me, sometimes for free, so I just couldn't say no. Sorry, mom." He began to cry. However, I was not falling for his tears anymore—I had no patience left.

"Do you know what a mess you made of the condo with the paint?" I asked.

"I didn't do anything with the paint. I just got there, did some drugs and sat down and fell asleep."

"That's it, get dressed and meet me in my car. We are going to the condo," I interrupted.

Kevin got in the car, and we silently drove the short distance to the condo. When we got there, I guided him to the front door and opened it. Unfortunately, it looked the same as it had early that morning.

Kevin looked around and turned white as a ghost. "I didn't do that to the walls!" he shouted.

"So, who do you think did? Larry and I have spent all our weekends for several weeks trying to get this condo ready to be put on the market and this is the thanks we get? I really don't even know how to tell Larry."

Wait, yes, I do, you are going to tell him today when he gets home from work," I told Kevin. My voice was high, and I was shaking.

Kevin spent most of the day in his bedroom, probably sleeping. Larry got home, and I told him that Kevin had something to tell him. I went and knocked on Kevin's door and told him Larry was home.

Larry sat down and waited for Kevin to come out of the bedroom.

"What's up?" Larry asked me.

"Kevin is going to tell you what he did last night, and it isn't good," I said.

"I messed up the condo with paint," Kevin quietly explained.

"I don't understand, when and how could you do this?" Larry asked.

"Well, I guess I was on drugs last night and went to the condo and thought I would help you guys out with the painting a little bit," Kevin said, almost defensively.

"Shit, I spent so much time there trying to help you out and this is what you do?" Larry grabbed his keys and said, "I'm going to see just what a mess he made of things."

"I'm going with you. I need to drive Kevin's car back anyway." I looked at Kevin and told him to stay right there until we returned.

23.

New rules: Kevin would be home directly from work, doing listed chores and would pay us $50.00 per week for room and board.

One afternoon, Kevin called me at work and asked if he could borrow $5,000.00 to buy a new car. Apparently, a nearby car salesman was up at the bar drinking and convinced Kevin that was a good idea and he would make him a good deal. Remember, Kevin has the mental capacity of a 16-year-old.

I told him no, that his car was completely fine, and he didn't need another one. So, he went to my mother and got the money. He told her that his car was old, and the inside was really trashed. Unfortunately, my mother did not call me first before she lent him the money. Two days later, he owned a new car.

So, Kevin was living with us, had a new car, two credit cards, which were probably maxed out, and no immediate good future, working in a restaurant/bar. This scenario went on for months. Though he was passing the drug tests that I would randomly give to him.

One night, I noticed that Kevin was still not home, and it was past midnight. I always left a kitchen light on that I could see from my bedroom. He was supposed to turn the light off when he got home so I knew all was well.

I stayed awake until I finally fell asleep. Suddenly, I was awakened by a noise in the kitchen. I got up, grabbed my robe, only to find Kevin fumbling around.

"What are you doing?" I asked.

"Making a bowl of cereal," he answered, as if it was the most normal thing to do at 4:00 am.

"Kevin, it's 4:00 am. Are you just getting home? What have you been doing all this time?" I softly yelled, as Larry was still asleep.

"Just hanging out with friends," he said, speaking naturally.

"You know you have a very strict curfew that you have broken tonight," I said sternly.

"And, we are having a big family party, which starts at noon, and I'm going to need your help getting everything ready." I whispered frantically.

"I'll help, I just need to eat a little bit," he said.

With that, I went back to bed and slept well, knowing that he was home and all right.

24.

I got up the next morning and began to clean the house and get ready for relatives to come over for Memorial Day. I never said anything to Larry about Kevin breaking his curfew. I was focused on getting the house and food prepared.

Suddenly, Larry came up from downstairs and quickly said, "Kevin is downstairs, TV is on, and I think he is asleep. There is cereal and milk all over the place. I turned off the TV; he seems dead to the world."

I ran downstairs, followed by Larry, to find Kevin slumped on the couch and indeed cereal and milk was everywhere. I just really had enough of him and his attitude. Mid-30s and still acting 16 was getting old to me.

"Kevin, get up!" I yelled, then again louder. I began to shake him and hit him with pillows. At one point, I held the pillow in my hands and pondered the thought of placing it over his head and ending all our problems. Luckily, instead, I called my brother who had been through stuff like this, and knew Kevin was fighting addiction.

"Call 911, right away!" he screamed.

"Are you sure?" I questioned.

"Yes, he might be in a coma," my brother said with fright in his voice.

So, I went back downstairs and called 911 and explained the situation. I'd hardly got off the phone when I heard sirens. Gone immediately were thoughts of a family party to prepare for.

Larry led the EMTs and police downstairs, a stretcher in tow. They asked me several questions about Kevin's health while they loaded him onto the stretcher. The EMTs said that they thought that Kevin was in a drug coma, and they were rushing him to the nearest emergency room.

I told Larry I was jumping in my car and following the ambulance. "Please talk to the police and clean up what you can downstairs and meet me at the hospital," I yelled.

Larry, in shock from everything that had happened, said that he watched the ambulance go down the street when one of the policemen came up to him.

"Sir, can you follow me, I want to show you something."

Larry said he and the policeman walked up to Kevin's 'new car' and looked inside.

"You see that?" the policeman pointed through the windows of Kevin's car.

Larry investigated the car; it was literally trashed inside. There were cut straws everywhere among fast food wrappers and partially eaten food. Larry became disgusted and almost literally sick to his stomach.

"If you clean this mess up within 30 minutes, when I come back, then I won't arrest your son for drug use and possession." He turned around and said that he would be back in 30 minutes. Thinking back, that had been incredibly nice of the policeman to do this.

Larry went inside and quickly came back out with cleaning supplies, a trash bag, and Kevin's keys. Meanwhile, I was speeding toward the hospital.

25.

When I arrived at the hospital, I quickly parked my car and headed toward the emergency room doors.

"What room is my son in? He came by ambulance just minutes ago. His name is Kevin Senger," I frantically questioned the nurse at the front desk.

When the nurse gave me the information, I ran down the hall toward his room. Upon entering the room, I found Kevin still in a coma and a nurse who was trying to start an IV. Suddenly, she jumped back and yelled, "Shit!" Kevin had involuntarily jerked his arm and stuck her with the needle.

"Do you want me to hold his arm?" I asked.

"I don't care what you do, I am not starting an IV on this drug addict. I may have HIV now." And she ran out of the room.

I stared at Kevin and wondered where I had gone wrong. Here was a 30-year-old man that was not supposed to live past the age of four. I didn't know what I would do without him. I had tried my hardest to be a good mom to him and raise him to be the best possible man. However, the problem was he wasn't a man. He was a 16-year-old boy trapped in a man's body. There was not one book that told me how to do this. I was on my own, trying to keep my son alive.

Another nurse appeared and asked me to leave for a little bit, so she could start the IV. By that time, Larry had appeared, and we walked to the waiting room together. He told me what the policeman said and how he had cleaned up the car perfectly. I thanked him for doing everything he had to do. I kept glancing back to Kevin's room hoping the nurse would leave his room so we could go in.

"Oh my God," I cried, "we need to call everyone that was supposed to come over today and tell them not to come. Just say that Kevin is in the hospital. Don't say why. Can you take care of this for me?" I asked. I hated asking Larry to do almost everything, but my mind was on Kevin.

"Of course, I'm on it," Larry said as he jumped up and headed toward the doors for some privacy while he called everyone.

I headed back to Kevin's emergency room. When I got there, the room was empty except for Kevin lying on the bed, motionless. The tears just started to flow from my eyes. I looked up to Heaven and whispered, "God, please help me raise this child. I don't know what I am doing and there is no manual to instruct me."

26.

The doctors and nurses sent Kevin to the ICU. He was in a drug-induced coma. He came to the hospital in a coma due to taking drugs. The doctors decided to induce him so he could come down from the drugs in a slow manner.

I found his room and came upon my little boy hooked up to multiple tubes and machines. They would only allow one person in his room at a time for just a few minutes. There was a nurse sitting in the room when I got there. She never left. I asked her if he needed that much attention, being that he was in a coma. She informed me that a nurse would be with him 24/7 for the length of his stay.

"But why?" I asked.

"Suicide watch," she replied. "Sometimes when they come out of the coma, they tend to start pulling out the tubes and purposely begin hurting themselves."

"How long will he be in a coma?" I asked.

"I can't say. You will have to speak with the doctor," she informed me and went back to her book.

I didn't ask when the doctor would be there, so I just sat down and held his hand until someone had the nerve to tell me to leave. The ICU only allowed one person at a time in the room for up to 15 minutes. I was planning on camping out in the waiting room so I could go in there during the 15-minute intervals. Finally, a doctor came in to speak with me.

"We will keep Kevin in a coma for five more days. This will allow his body to recover from the tragic incident," the doctor said. I noticed that he had said 'incident' and not 'accident'.

"A specialized psychologist will be by before he is discharged to help you understand the process," he explained.

A psychologist? Why would we need one of those? Larry had called Brian in Texas, and he took the first flight home to be with us; there was nowhere else he wanted to be. All I told people was that he was in intensive care but would not tell them why. I kept that a very guarded secret.

27.

Larry picked up Brian from the airport. Brian, being a doctor, ignored the one-person rule and entered Kevin's room and headed right toward me with an all-encompassing hug. When he let me go, he casually looked over at Kevin in the bed and back at me, then left the room to look at Kevin's chart. I saw him just shake his head.

"You know, Mom, I came up here for you," he whispered.

"Why? Kevin is the one in a coma and hurting," I explained.

"You are hurting, and he did this to you. He was very selfish with his actions, not caring about who he hurt. He has always been that way," Brian said.

I pushed myself away from Brian in disbelief that he would think this and say it out loud to me. I left Kevin's room and practically ran out the door to get some air. So much had happened within such a short period of time that I found myself trembling.

The past few days, everyone expressed their sympathies to me, not seeming to care that Kevin was hurt. I didn't understand. I just kept going round and round in my head… Kevin was the one hurting, feel sorry for him.

The next day, a psychologist came into the room and introduced himself. He explained that Kevin needed to go from the hospital to an all-inclusive in-house treatment center for addicts of all kinds. Kevin would be there for at least one week, then be an outpatient for an extended amount of time.

The doctor suggested, in the meantime, that I clean his room of all things that would remind him of using drugs.

The next day, Kevin would be coming out of the coma, and the suicide-watch nurse would be with him until he left the hospital to go to the treatment facility. The following day, an ambulance would take Kevin to the treatment center, and I was to follow him by car. I would be meeting with the team and doing his in-take.

This was happening so fast; a few weeks ago, we were all doing our own thing and everything was fine, or so I thought…NOT. I know that now. I was taking a crash course in drug use and abuse.

I went home and entered Kevin's room, deciding to look through his desk drawers. I found three driving tickets and one parking ticket, all issued in North County. North County is a very dangerous place to be. I called the traffic clerk and told her what happened. She said that the parking ticket was in a residential area, and he had just parked his car in the middle of the street. She forgave all but $50.00 of the $275.00 he had accumulated. This was where he was getting most of his drugs. How did he even know people in North County, let alone that it was unsafe to be there alone?

28.

The next morning, I ate breakfast and then headed to the hospital. When I entered Kevin's room, I was surprised to find him sitting up eating breakfast.

"Well, good morning, and welcome back from the dead," I happily said to him.

"Hi mom. Can you tell me why I am in the hospital?" he asked.

Although I was somewhat shocked by his question, I went through everything with him slowly so he could comprehend and understand it. I also told him that later in the day he would be going to the rehab facility. He nodded and let it slowly sink in. I just kept staring at him in amazement that he had done what he did and survived.

As planned, the nurse came in to get him ready for the transport. She said he would stay in his hospital gown and change into street clothes when he arrived. She also told me to take all his things back home except for his shoes, which she was helping him put on, minus the shoelaces. Within minutes, the men from the ambulance transport showed up, gave me the address and told me to follow them. I would need to give the facility information. I called Larry at work to see if he could meet us. I felt that I would need him to help me fill in the blanks.

29.

I pulled into the substance abuse facility that I never knew was there. As I entered, I asked someone where Kevin was and all they told me was that someone would be out to get me soon. I saw Larry enter the building and I rushed to meet him. He could tell that I was trembling as he hugged me tightly.

After about 20 minutes, I noticed that Kevin was being wheeled down a hallway on a gurney, still in his hospital gown and with only his shoes on. I started to follow but was stopped by the person we were with. We then went into a small room. This is where they did the intake for patients. After answering all the questions that we could, they handed us a couple of brochures to read. We were told that he would be there for about a week for intense therapy. Larry and I were allowed to see him one time, midway, and then again when we picked him up. Since he arrived there without clothes, I was told to bring him underwear and clothes for a week, and to drop them off as soon as possible so he could get out of the hospital gown.

"Can't I see him now to say goodbye?" I implored.

"No, no communication. He doesn't have a cell phone anyway. No visits, and when you do come, you will be searched for contraband."

I felt like Kevin had just entered prison. I'm sure he felt the same way. I thought to myself, how dare they tell me when I can see my son and when I can't? But I also knew that Kevin was where he needed to be. I just hoped they would take good care of him.

Larry and I left, bewildered and confused. We had been thrust into a world that we knew nothing about but were learning fast.

30.

I went up to the facility the next morning to deliver Kevin some clothes. When I got there, even though I knew the answer, I asked to see Kevin. My heart leaped when the nurse behind the counter looked at the computer, but then she said I could see him in two days. She took the clothes from me, and I turned around and left. I wondered if Kevin was looking out a window and seeing me pull out of the parking lot. Did he feel betrayed?

The next two days at work, all I did was go through the motions. At night, Larry and I mindlessly watched TV. It didn't do any good to talk about Kevin. There was nothing we could do.

Wednesday night, Larry and I met up after work at the facility. We asked to see Kevin and the nurse, again, looked at the computer and said for us to have a seat and someone would be out to get us. We turned around to see a few other people waiting to see their loved ones. We waited, looking around at nothing until finally our name was called. We followed a young man in hospital garb to a small break room, where other people gathered visiting with their loved ones, at different tables. It indeed felt like a prison.

Finally, Kevin appeared. He looked lost and confused. I waited until he got closer, then hugged him with everything I had. We sat down and I asked what sort of things he had been doing. He said that he shared his room with another guy, they went to classes, group therapy, exercised, and had private counseling. I asked him how everything was going and all he said, in a soft voice, was, "Okay" and "When can I come home?"

We talked for a while longer, just about things at home and what we had been doing, and then it was time for us to go, hugs and tears all around. We said we would be back on Saturday to pick him up, and we watched him disappear into the hallway. It took everything in me not to follow him, turn him around, and have him follow us out the door.

On Saturday, we got up early and rushed to the facility to get Kevin. When we got there, a doctor came out and led us to a small room for a conversation to say that Kevin was free from drugs now. He also said that Kevin cooperated in group and individual counseling. I asked him if he could share with us any insights as to why he'd been doing drugs.

"No, it is all confidential, especially since Kevin is an adult, but he now has the tools to help him through his urges. I will tell you this: he will be back—they always come back," the doctor said.

I looked him straight in the eye and said sternly, "Then you didn't do your job right. He will not be back." Kevin appeared then, and we drove home.

31.

On the way home from the facility, we told Kevin that we had his new car repossessed, and he no longer had that good job at the restaurant with insurance. He was now at the bottom starting his life again. He just looked down and nodded.

Kevin was instructed to go to the facility for two-hour outpatient therapy, once a week. He was also supposed to attend a one-hour session with AA once a week. Since I had to work, these occurred in the evening. We had his car repossessed, which meant that I would have to drive him everywhere.

So, two nights a week, we went to the facility for his outpatient therapy and once a week for a local AA meeting. This all took a large chunk out of my life, but if it helped Kevin not to be tempted by drugs, then it was worth it. Luckily, it was light in the evening, and I was able to take a book and read while I waited.

In addition to all that, Kevin managed to get a job without my prodding him and all on his own, at a nearby grocery store during the day. His hours had to coincide with mine, since he would be using my car. Luckily, the store allowed Kevin to make his own hours. No more restaurants or bars. Unbeknownst to me, however, he was online trying to find a girlfriend. As if we didn't have enough going on in our lives!

32.

Kevin found a girl online, who had a small son. He met up with her and it seemed to be going well. One night, before he borrowed my car to go see her, I asked him if he was transparent with her about his history.

"Yes, I told her about my past drug problem," he volunteered.

"And what was her response?" I inquired.

"She said I can't do or have any drugs in her apartment or car, or wherever her son is around. She adopted her son and if social services would make a surprise visit and find drugs of any kind, they would take away her child. She is very strict about that," Kevin explained.

Great, I thought, she would watch over him when I couldn't. After a few months, we got him a cheap small car that he could go back and forth to meetings with, go to his job, and see his girlfriend, Wendy. This was a relief to me, as driving him back and forth to places was getting old.

It didn't take very much time at all before Kevin moved in with Wendy and her 4-year-old son. It was a heavy sigh of relief, but I had a feeling that things were going very fast. Supposedly, he was still going to his AA meetings, but was finished with his out-patient therapy sessions. One thing about Wendy: she tolerated no lying from Kevin, so he had to be honest with her as to where he was going once a week in the evenings.

I was a little unsure how Kevin was going to deal with Wendy's 4-year-old son, as he was never around little kids. But I had forgotten that he was just a kid himself, mentally, so the mental age gap was minimal. This went smoothly, as far as I knew, for about four months before he came to me with a concerning statement.

"I'm going to ask Wendy to marry me," Kevin proudly exclaimed. I was really surprised to hear this after only four months of dating.

"Are you sure? Is this coming from you or her?" I asked.

"We both want to get married," Kevin said.

That statement told me everything that I needed to know. Wendy wanted to get married. She saw a future with Kevin as a stepfather for her son and monetary support for her. I'm sure marriage had never crossed Kevin's 16-year-old mind.

The next time they both came over for dinner, I took Wendy aside and explained to her Kevin's background, mentally and physically. I wanted to make sure that she knew exactly what she was getting into and that what she saw was what she got. Things with Kevin would not change.

"But that's okay, I just love him and he's good with Jon. It will work out fine," Wendy said hopefully, trying to convince me, which she did not.

So, Kevin decided that he would ask Wendy to a St. Louis Cardinal's baseball game one night in May, get a hotel room downtown, and then ask her to marry him. He had gotten a cheap, nice enough ring to give her. Not an easy feat because her ring size was 12.

The big day arrived. After the game, where they drank and ate things paid for by Kevin, they went to check into the hotel. Kevin had one credit card and he checked ahead of time to make sure the daily rate of the hotel was on his credit card. What he didn't figure in were taxes and hotel fees. Yep, he was short $45.00. Luckily, Wendy had a credit card that would cover this. Red flags were popping up everywhere for me regarding this situation.

33.

Of course, she said 'yes.' The planning of the wedding began. We only had three months to arrange everything and pay for it all —the rehearsal dinner and the wedding/reception. Wendy's parents weren't paying for anything because it was her second marriage. We had paid for Brian's wedding/reception, so I didn't have a problem with it. Brian and his family were coming up from Texas to St. Louis for the wedding and helping to get everything together.

The date was 10/10/2010. Wendy selected that date because she figured that Kevin would never forget it that way. In the beginning of August, just two months before the wedding, Kevin called me with a problem. He proceeded to tell me that technically,

Wendy was still married. Wendy and her husband had not lived together for four years, but neither bothered to get a final divorce because the idea of remarriage never came up. I was very upset. First, for her to be so stupid not to realize she was still married, and second, all the money I had put into this wedding while there was a chance of it not happening. Somehow, Wendy was able to speak with a judge and got a "quicky" divorce just in time.

Nani and Kevin at Kevin's wedding

The big day came. Since neither of them were religious, we had a pastor come to the wedding venue and it all took place in one area. Everything was going well. Unbeknownst to me, Wendy's mother, who lived in Florida and came up for the wedding, said to Wendy, "You know you can do better than him, don't you?" right as she was beginning to walk down the aisle. Then, her 4-year-old son refused to walk her down the aisle. Wendy had spoiled that child immensely. Her father stepped in and told him that if he didn't do what he was told, he would take him out to the car and spank him. That did the trick.

The reception was very nice, except Kevin was so happy and talking to people that he never got around to eating, and when he went back to the table, all the food had been taken away. The reception lasted several hours. Next, we all went to a park to take pictures, and Kevin and Wendy could open their gifts. This seemed so strange to me, opening gifts in a parking lot in front of everyone.

Brian and his family left the next day and things seemed to return to normal. Because Kevin had had testicular cancer, he needed a shot of testosterone weekly, or he would physically return to an age before puberty. Wendy was now responsible for giving Kevin his shots.

34.

One Sunday in the spring, I decided that I wanted to take the entire family on a week's cruise for Christmas. This was something that I had always wanted to do. Of course, Kevin, Wendy and Jake, Wendy's son, were in on it and when I approached Brian, he wanted to go as well. All the plans were made; all we had to do was wait for Christmastime. It was great not having to buy gifts for everyone.

We met in New Orleans the day before the cruise was set to sail, to make sure that we were there and ready to go. Brian and his family flew in from Texas and we drove nine hours to meet them at the hotel. Brian paid for his family's staterooms and tours, and we paid for everything else. Of course, Kevin and

Wendy paid for nothing. I should have known that being Christmas, the cruise would be full of families with small children. We made the best of it, and we all went on our ways, and then met up for dinner. The last day on one of the islands, we all went on different tours. While Larry and I were walking back to the ship after our tour, we happened to see Kevin, Jake, and Wendy in front of us, and Wendy appeared to be limping.

Apparently, on their tour, it was stated that tennis shoes were highly recommended, and to stay on the cleared path while walking, not to venture on the mossy, rocky grass. Wendy thought that the people in front of them were walking too slow, so she went around them, which took her onto the mossy rocks. She wanted Kevin and Jake to follow her, but they declined because the guide had advised them against doing so. Within a minute or two, she had slid on the moss and down she went. Wendy was not a small person—she was six feet tall and about 270 pounds. As such, she fell hard.

We continued to walk with them back to the ship and into the hospital for X-rays. It had been hours and she still had not been taken care of. I guess emergency rooms are as slow on the sea as they are on land.

Our dinner time was approaching, and we still had to get cleaned up and changed. So, we left them there and went to dinner with the rest of the family. About an hour later, here comes Kevin, Wendy and Jake, with Wendy in a wheelchair. Apparently, she had scrapes and bruises and a possible broken wrist. Her wrist was put in a cast, but she also said that her knee was hurting, though they could not find anything wrong with it. The next day, we were at sea before we disembarked for New Orleans. Poor Kevin had to do everything for Wendy as well as push her from place to place. This was Kevin's last day of fun on the cruise.

The ship docked, we said our goodbyes, and Brian and his family flew back to San Antonio while Larry got our van from the parking lot. The 9-hour trip stretched out to 11 hours because we had to stop so often for Wendy to get out to stretch and complain.

35.

Kevin was now working at a hospital, cleaning and sterilizing operating instruments, while Wendy worked at a healthcare college. Together, they were making a very good salary. Kevin's boss informed him that he needed to be certified to continue working in that department and then he would be able to get raises. To be certified, he needed to take a very involved test. I was worried because of Kevin's learning disabilities. He studied the book on his own, and a few weeks later he took the test. Unfortunately, he failed, though he had two more chances to pass. He knew how to do his job, but the test also involved clerical duties, which he had never done and never would do, plus different ways of doing things, which made it difficult for him to learn.

Kevin, always the funny man.

Larry thought maybe flash cards would work, so Kevin came over to work with Larry for three straight weeks. Kevin then took the test a second time but failed it again. He only had one more chance to pass the certification exam before he lost his job at the hospital. So, he went online and found a site that had a practice exam, and every day, Kevin would come home and run through the practice test.

The time and day had arrived for his last chance. I told him to call me as soon as he knew something. After you take the test, the computer automatically calculates the score and lets you know if you have been successful.

My phone rang at about 2:00 pm. It was Kevin.

"Hey, what's up?" I said lightly.

"Well, mom, I guess I'll be looking for another job," Kevin said sadly.

"It's okay honey, I will help you," I reassured him. Then it got quiet.

"Mom, I passed the test!"

36.

As far as I knew, things between Kevin and Wendy had been going along well. So, I was surprised when they both came over one day and said they needed to talk to me.

To begin, Wendy told me that she quit her job at the college because she didn't agree with the dean, when in fact, I later learned that she had been fired because she would tell people she was visiting other campuses, when she would go home to nap. It finally caught up with her when another facility spoke with the dean.

So, they were down to one salary. Wendy told me she had an interview with the Red Cross the next week.

"So, why, other than that, did you need to speak with me?" I asked.

They both looked at each other and then Wendy said, "We would like for you to set us up on a budget."

This surprised me, because although Kevin could not handle the simple concept of money, I was sure that Wendy could. Kevin then dumped a grocery bag full of bills onto the table. After sifting through them— credit card bills, doctor bills, hospital bills and medicine bills, and bills they needed to pay back from family and friends—I just sat back and shook my head. Apparently, they loved to eat out, buy whatever they wanted, and live the lifestyle that others only dreamt about. Without adding it up, the guess was that they were about $50,000.00 in debt.

With only Kevin's salary now, it was clearly impossible to make ends meet, let alone pay back all their debt. So, I made them a budget based on Kevin's salary and Wendy's unemployment. They didn't like it at all. In fact, they called me the 'budget Nazi!' Keep in mind, they came to me. They were angry that they couldn't go out to eat, go to the movies, or buy whatever they wanted. It was like working with toddlers.

I made copies of all their debt and gave the originals back to them and sent them on their way. Wendy oversaw making sure the budget was met. Her interview at the Red Cross had been successful and she got the job. The pay was about half of what she'd been making at the college, so even though she was now working, the budget was still more than tight.

37.

Wendy's job at the Red Cross lasted only three weeks. She said that she couldn't carry or set up the tables when they went on sight for blood drives. So back to unemployment she went. Another few weeks went by with them affording food and rent, but little else. Their bills were not being paid. This really bothered me, so we lent them money to pay for some of them. BIG MISTAKE.

After about two months, Wendy got a job at a Mercy doctor's office as an MA (medical assistant), to which she'd been certified for at college. Now hopefully the bills will be paid. Kevin and Wendy told me how much their take-home pay would be, and I would tell them which bills to pay and how much.

Now, I was really referred to as the budget Nazi. This budgeting occurred every week, since Kevin was paid one week and Wendy the next.

Wendy has had diabetes since she was a teenager, but somehow, she can't control it, and so she had an insulin pump inserted to help regulate it. When her blood sugar gets low, she is just supposed to press the pump and it will correct it. Wendy continued to have diabetic incidents, though, such as falling, going to sleep, or slipping into a semi-coma. The doctor told her to lose weight and stop eating sweets. Luckily, when her son got older and was home, she would call out to him to bring her a cookie or piece of candy when her blood sugar dropped. If Kevin wasn't home, she would call Kevin at work to come home. As an adult, I could not understand why she had so much trouble controlling it. Kevin then enlightened me of the fact that she ate cookies, candy, and cake whenever she felt like it. Each episode left her with a migraine, which caused her to call in sick to work. At her job, you accrued sick time and vacation time based on the hours worked. Wendy seldom worked a five-day week, so when she called in sick, she didn't get paid. There went the established budget. Wendy was also on so many prescription drugs, that that alone ate up more than half of the budget.

By this time, Kevin was getting tired of being frequently called home from work. As with Wendy, if he didn't work, he didn't get paid. It wasn't that he lacked empathy, which I had to teach him because it didn't come naturally, it was the fact that her incompetence appeared to be self-inflicted. Wendy was doing this to herself when she obviously knew better but lacked maturity and self-control. Plus, when this happened, Wendy got attention.

38.

As the years went by, Kevin and Wendy's fighting became worse. Wendy would always call me to complain about Kevin, what he was or was not doing to her satisfaction. What did she hope to accomplish by calling her husband's mother? She wanted the attention that Kevin never seemed to give her, more hugs, handholding, and listening. I reminded Wendy that I told her what she was getting before they got married.

Then it dawned on me that Kevin had never been taught to be a husband, plus he was only 16 years of age mentally. It did not occur to him to hold her hand, comfort her when she needed it, or just converse with her about her feelings. Wendy was extra needy, and he didn't have a clue how to handle it. I sat him down several times to help him understand Wendy's needs.

Brian and Kevin watching their favorite team play, The St. Louis Blues.

While all of this was going on, Larry and I had to supplement their lack of income. I see now that this was a severe mistake. I became the worst enabler as far as Kevin was concerned. Larry was so sweet and understanding, although, most of the time he didn't know how much I had lent to them. Then one day, by sheer accident, I found out that Kevin was going to Brian for money. Brian would do anything for his brother, so he would also supplement his income. This was only putting a Band-Aid on an open wound, and Wendy would eat whatever she wanted despite her diabetes. Soon, Kevin got tired of talking to her about it and thus, Wendy would miss more and more days from work because she had headaches or her back hurt or anything else she could come up with. Meanwhile, Kevin's paycheck was the only dependable source of income.

One day, Larry's company folded, leaving him without a job. We could survive on my salary, but it was very tight. It also meant that we could not contribute anymore to Kevin and Wendy's budget.

Within weeks, Larry found another job, but we needed to catch up on our bills before we gave any more money to Kevin and Wendy. Wendy always said that she never wanted to talk about finances with her parents—it just wasn't any of their business—so they never contributed any of their money or knew how bad Kevin and Wendy were financially.

Wendy's company decided that they wanted a few people to work from home, and since Wendy answered phones and was not seeing patients anymore, she was one of the employees that was selected. I thought this was a great idea, as she wouldn't be apt to miss so many days of work. Years ago, Wendy had asked her doctor to sign a form stating that her diabetes made her disabled. With that paper in hand, she gave it to her boss. Under the Missouri Disability Act, no employer could fire her for missing so many days of work for diabetic reasons.

Working from home was okay for a week or two, but then she started back up with different things that stopped her from going from her bed to the living room where her work computer was.

Understandably, Kevin was furious since he was seeing one hundred percent of his paycheck ng toward paying bills and no money left over to have fun or go out to eat. One day, he came home and there was a new bedspread on the bed. He asked where it had come from, and Wendy said that she saw it online and liked it, so she borrowed her stepmom's Amazon card.

"Great," Kevin said, "Now that will be another bill we will have to pay for."

"We don't have to give her the money for it until the bill comes in," Wendy said, attempting to justify the purchase. With that said, Kevin went out to his car and left.

39.

The Amazon bills were coming every month, as if it were a monthly bill. These ranged from $250.00 to $500.00 per month that was owed to Ruth, Wendy's stepmom, as soon as she got the bill, no exceptions.

Wendy always had an excuse because she had to buy the things she did. I put some of the blame on Ruth for letting Wendy charge things to her account. Her parents had no idea they couldn't afford anything. To help combat this, as I would write out the budget, I always put the Amazon bill at the end if there was any money left. Wendy would complain that her stepmom needed the money before her bill came in, and I would say "Where do you want me to get it from?"

Every month, the same thing happened. Somehow, we got the bill paid, but it was always late. Wendy, however, produced a solution. Kevin needed to get a second job. Since he got home at 11:00 pm and did not have to be at work again until 2:00 pm, he could get a job working mornings. So, Kevin applied for a job working at The Dollar Tree. He would work there 4-5 days per week. He also needed to wear khaki pants and a green button-down shirt, which he had neither and had to buy them. Making minimum wage, buying two sets of uniforms, and working just a few hours a day totaled up to not being a very good idea.

He would empty the truck when it arrived at the store and stock shelves. We all agreed that the money Kevin made would go toward paying off credit card bills. Kevin worked these two jobs for about three months before he said that he had to quit The Dollar Tree because his feet were hurting so bad, and he was not getting used to it. He was on his feet all day at the hospital and then again on his feet at The Dollar Tree. Wendy did not like this, but what could she do?

Wendy was about 120 pounds overweight. This was not good because of her diabetes, so she decided to have a gastric bypass done. She had her doctor sign a statement that because of her diabetes, she needed the surgery to lose weight. I asked her how much time she would be off from work, and she said probably two weeks. Luckily, she could work from home. However, how were they going to pay bills, which were already overdue, with Wendy's paychecks missing? So, Larry suggested that they file for bankruptcy.

In addition to their rent, two car payments, insurance, gas, food, medicine and medical bills, they had 12 credit cards that were all maxed out. This budget was stressing me out. Larry kept saying to give it back to them to do. But if I did that, they would be in much worse shape, if that were even possible. Bankruptcy was the only reasonable option. Wendy's dad, however, said that it would ruin their credit for about seven years if they did not have more than $15,000.00 in debt, but it did not make sense—they were in debt for around $50,000.00. He knew nothing, because Wendy refused to tell her parents how bad off they were. They already had poor credit and by just making the minimum payments the problem was not going to go away any time soon.

Then Wendy had a great idea: to do a consolidation loan. This would take care of their credit cards and collection calls. However, they still had medical bills, medicine, food, Amazon, car payments, insurance, rent, and now one large bill for the consolidation loan.

Two things happened with the company that Wendy found for the loan: one, that it did not stop the collection calls, and two, only a fraction of each bill was being paid and the company did not acknowledge when the bills were due, so late fees and overdraft charges were being tacked on after the company paid themselves.

While this was going on, Wendy, after fully recovering from her surgery, was still only working 2-3 days a week, and Kevin was getting frustrated.

Kevin and Wendy had been married for 10 years. In those years, Jake, Wendy's son, was turning into a teenager. Wendy was 'hot and cold' with him. One minute she was screaming at him and the next she was apologizing and hugging him. During this turmoil, she would always turn to Kevin and ask him to support her. I never trained Kevin to be a dad, so he was a little lost. He would tell Jake not to fight with his mom, but that got nowhere. Jake didn't respect Kevin and never did anything Kevin asked him to do, so the screaming continued, usually ending when Jake went into his room and slammed the door. Wendy would then turn on Kevin. Kevin could see both sides, so he was mentally unable to help, plus he hated confrontation.

40.

While Kevin was at work one night, Wendy called me and said that while Kevin had been in the shower, she decided to look at the contents on his phone. She found that he was texting girls online, several of them. I was shocked, first by the fact that she would look at his phone and second that she would call me and tell me this. I am not the third wheel in their marriage. Instead of waiting for him to come home to discuss it, she asked him while he'd been working—hardly the time or the place. But Kevin told her he didn't know why he was doing it and that he would stop.

Remember, we are referring to a 16-year-old mentality. My family and friends had been telling me that Kevin acts differently when Wendy is not around, that she is always putting him down and making fun of him. I guess I chose not to acknowledge it.

The girls online were complimenting him, listening to him, and confirming that he was indeed a man, all in exchange for money. These girls would use sob stories and ask Kevin to send them anywhere from ten dollars to hundreds of dollars. This is money that Kevin just did not have to send, so when the girls found this out, they quit talking to him and he would move on to the next girl that he found would talk to him. He was able to send tiny amounts of money from time to time. This was a whole different world for me: Catfishing.

Kevin and Wendy had a serious talk about the situation. He said he was sorry he'd hurt her feelings, that he would not do it again, and that she was free to look at his phone at any time.

All was quiet for a few months when I got another call from Wendy. This time, Kevin was home. He was on the couch texting a girl from Arkansas, when Wendy got suspicious and yanked the phone away from him. She texted the girl and told her who she was, and that Kevin was married and to leave him alone. The girl said she knew where Kevin lived, giving the address of where he lived and worked, and she was leaving right then to get Kevin, and if necessary, to beat Wendy up for the way she treated him.

I told Wendy that this was not going to happen. Kevin, of course, said that he was sorry. He enjoyed the attention and for a while, took him away from his real-life situation. I suggested that she take away his phone for a week and clear everything off his contact list that they both didn't know and to go through Facebook and block any of the girls that he had spoken with, which she did.

41.

Life went on. I was not happy that I could not speak with Kevin when I wanted or needed to, but I felt one week without the distraction of his phone would work. Immediately after she took the phone away, she sent out a text to everyone on her and his contact list that she had taken Kevin's phone away and if anyone needed to speak with him to call her. There were only a few family members and close friends that needed to know this, not over 82 people, most of which were her own contacts. Brian sent Wendy an email, stating,

"Tell Kevin when he gets out of phone jail to call me."

It was a joke, but people on the contact list thought Kevin really was in jail. This misunderstanding caused an array of emails and messages going back and forth. Wendy went to Kevin's work after a few days and presented him with his phone, a grand gesture on her part.

As weeks went on, it became exceedingly difficult to make ends meet for Kevin and Wendy. I could never make a budget work without starving them with their food allowance, even though they had a consolidation loan, which I'd convinced the company to break down the enormous one-month payment into two somewhat double payments. The creditors kept calling them both all the time. Plus, Wendy never worked a full week. Finally, Kevin called me and asked if he could stay with us for about a week. He and Wendy were constantly fighting, and he could not take it anymore. I checked with Larry, and we agreed that it might not be a bad idea.

The week went by fast. Kevin went to and from work. He pitched in around the house and was quiet. Five days went by, and Wendy called me to see, from my point of view, how Kevin was doing. Apparently, she had been speaking with him and he seemed remorseful and ready to go home. I said to her that he seemed quiet and sullen.

"You've been giving Kevin his testosterone shots once a week, right?" I asked Wendy.

"Well, sometimes I forgot; come to think of it, he hasn't had a shot for a few weeks," Wendy admitted. "Even with insurance, the vials are expensive. By the way, we still owe my stepmom $425.00 for the things I ordered on Amazon," she added.

I went ballistic.

"You have not given him his shot on a regular once a week basis? I can understand Kevin forgetting the first time, but thereafter he begins slipping back in his mental age. You told me that you had it all set up on a calendar, which was in plain view and in the kitchen. This tells me that you are a very controlling person." And I hung up.

42.

Wendy and Larry had been fighting for some time. The main reason was because of Jake, Wendy's son. Every year, since Jake had been in 8th grade, Larry had been helping him with his math homework. Wendy said that no one in her family was smart enough to help him because they did not understand math. So, Monday through Friday Wendy would text Larry with the homework, and he would do it after coming home from work. This would take some time, because it had been over 40 years since Larry had done high school math, and it was different from what he knew. Each night was spent doing homework for about two hours. Larry also sent how to do the problems along with the answers so hopefully Jake could learn.

Larry's job needed him to go to Colorado Springs, Colorado, for some major all-day training for a period of six weeks. Wendy had the nerve to expect Larry, after a day's training, staying in a hotel room, to continue to do Jake's math. I told him absolutely not, but Larry, who has a heart of gold, did it anyway.

The final limit was when Larry found out that Wendy was just writing down the answers while Jake was playing video games. This was the end of the year with only one month left of the school year.

Larry said, "Enough is enough," and refused to do anymore after four years' worth of Jake not learning anything. Wendy had a fit over this and said that Jake would probably not graduate unless he passed math. But Larry said he did not care, he was done.

Next thing we knew, Kevin was on the phone pleading with Larry to do Jake's homework for his sake, as Larry heard Wendy yelling in the background. Larry thought about it, listening to Wendy cussing Kevin out in the background, and finally agreed to do it. However, he told Kevin that he did not want to see Wendy or Jake ever again.

43.

My extended family felt the same way about Wendy and Jake as we did. So, she was not invited to any birthday parties, holiday events, or even our grandson's wedding, which was taking place in New Orleans. This was hard on Kevin and Wendy's marriage.

On January 2nd, I got a text from Kevin that said he needed to talk to me in person and asked if I could meet him after he got off work at a certain restaurant. Of course, I agreed to meet up with him.

Kevin and I met at the restaurant. As I watched him eat, I kept wondering what the meeting was all about. Finally, when he was ¾ of the way done with his meal, I asked him what he wanted to talk to me about.

"Mom, I just cannot take it anymore. All Wendy and I do is fight, and if we're not fighting with each other, one of us is fighting with Jake. She never works a full week, so we are getting further and further behind in our bills. I can only work so much overtime to pay the bills." Tears started to well up in his eyes. I figured this was what he wanted to discuss.

"So, what do you have planned?" I asked, knowing the answer.

"Can I come live with you and Larry for a little bit until I get my own place?" Kevin asked.

"If this is what you want to do, then of course, you can live with us," I reassured him. He got up and gave me an enormous hug.

"I'm going home now to tell Wendy and to pack up my clothes, then I will be over."

We said our 'see you soon' goodbyes in the parking lot, and I headed home to get the guest room ready and give Larry a heads up. But I knew I did not have to check with Larry first because he loves both of my boys with all his heart and is extremely easygoing.

Around 7:00 pm, the front door opened and in walked Kevin with his packed clothes. The dogs went crazy! As we hugged, I noticed his eyes were red from crying.

"How did it go?" I asked.

"Well, I got home and started packing my things. Wendy asked me what I was doing. I told her that I could not live like this anymore. She kept asking 'what did I do?' so I told her that she never works, so all of the bills fall on me to pay, she treats me like a kid, she gets mad at me when she and Jake fight and I don't step in, she monitors everything I do when I am not with her, and she looks at my phone constantly. With that, I finished packing without another word," Kevin explained.

While all of this was going on, Brian and his wife were getting a divorce after 30 years of marriage. Brian wanted the marriage to continue to work because of the children. However, his wife made this desire impossible. For his own mental stability, Brian chose to move out and start divorce proceedings. Brian is an internist and has been working at a practice that he is part ownership of. Again, this was more than all right with the rest of the family, because from almost the beginning, no one had liked her. She was abrasive and mean and it just got worse as the years went on. However, this union produced two beautiful children, my grandchildren, whom I cherished with everything I had.

It wasn't long before Brian met a woman named Jeanine. She was exactly the opposite of Brian's first wife. Brian had somewhat of a hard time accepting her warmth and compassion because he just wasn't used to it.

Brian had a best friend from college, John, who was also an internist. He had a practice in Dallas that was going quite well. He has always wanted Brian to go into partnership with him, but Brian didn't want to leave San Antonio where his life had been for over 25 years. John suggested that Brian move up to Dallas to get away from always running into his ex-wife. He talked it over with his Fiancé and they both decided it would be a good idea. Brian and John drew up the paperwork, so they were both on the same page and nothing was left for future discussion. So, Brian and Jeanine packed up and moved to Dallas to start a completely new life.

So, both boys were going through life changes at about the same time.

44.

Kevin had no sooner got to our house when Wendy texted him asking when he was going to get the rest of his stuff. He told her soon and that he would let her know when. She told him that she would box up what she could. So, Wendy went from 'please don't leave me' to 'I am packing up all your things.'

I did impose a few rules for Kevin while he was living under my roof again. "First, you must be home by midnight, otherwise I will worry about you. Second, when you do your laundry, do not leave the house until you complete it. Keep your bedroom and bathroom clean and do not leave food anywhere the dogs can get it. And last, you must give us rent every week." Not too bad, I thought. Of course, he agreed to everything.

Kevin filed for divorce on February 2nd. He agreed to pay all the bills for January and half of February, then just take over his own bills, and Wendy would have to pay her own. If she worked full time, she and Kevin would make the same salary. He asked for nothing in the divorce except his personal items and she could keep everything else. He just wanted out of that toxic marriage.

Kevin's stepsister, Sara, was getting married at the end of February and Kevin was excited to go. He and Sara had a good relationship. Steve, the boys' father, basically ignores him, but Kevin is persistent—I don't know why. I tried to think of ways he could meet different people, and this seemed to be the beginning.

The big day arrived. Kevin was excited to see his stepsister, Sara, and his father again. Fast forward to the next morning when he came into the kitchen grinning from ear to ear.

"Did you have fun?" I asked, wanting to hear all about it.

"Yep. In fact, I met a girl. I knew her from before when I used to hang out with Sara, but I was married then. So, we sat together and hung out. We are going to go out on Friday night. Since she lives in St. Clair, MO, about 30 miles away, she is going to pick me up," he informed us.

"Sounds good. Go slow, you are just getting out of a relationship, and you are not divorced yet," I cautioned.

Over a months' time, Linda, his new girlfriend, and Kevin were getting close. Although he told me that they had not had sex yet, he would spend all his free time there.

One day, Kevin texted me, 'What is administrated leave?' I asked what it was all about, and he said that he would fill me in when he got home, four hours earlier than usual.

We sat down at the kitchen table, and he said that his boss came in and said, "Stop what you are doing—you are now on administrative leave until further notice, go home now.' This was Wednesday.

For the past three weeks, Kevin had been going to work early and staying late to pick up the slack from a co-worker who broke his leg and could not work for a while. So, between extra work, traveling an extra 30 miles from Linda's house and watching movies until all hours of the night, Kevin was beginning to make mistakes. He worked at the same job doing the same thing at the same hospital for 15 years. But he was starting to make mistakes.

On Friday, his boss called and said that HR wanted to fire him, so he said to come in and clean out his locker. He also said to let him know when he was going to do this, so they could have security lead him in and out. I explained to Kevin that this happened for several reasons, and I proceeded to tell him why it happened from my perspective.

A day later, I pulled into the driveway and saw a girl standing outside by the front door, texting. I assumed it was Linda and introduced myself. She also introduced herself to me, all the while texting. She said that Kevin was inside talking to his boss. Next thing we knew, Kevin came out the front door and said, "Well, I just got fired over the phone because of some mistakes that I made. I have been there for 15 years." I told him he was making those mistakes because he was tired, and I looked at Linda.

45.

When Larry called on his way home from work, I explained to him what had happened to Kevin at work. He said when he got home, he would speak with Kevin.

Larry arrived, gave the dogs some love, then went into Kevin's room to maybe find out more of what happened. About 30 minutes later, Larry and Kevin came into the kitchen. Larry sat down on his computer and helped Kevin fill out his unemployment paperwork and write a resume.

Once Kevin placed his resume online, he immediately received phone calls. Kevin, being certified in what he does, was valuable in the medical field. Most calls were recruiters looking for travelers—

people who would travel from state to state for a period, wherever a hospital was short-staffed. I did not think that Kevin would be able to mentally handle this, then a recruiter called looking to fill a job at Shriners Hospital for Children in St. Louis. It would be a contract for six months. I had to explain what a hiring contract was to Kevin.

Kevin went to the interview and immediately clicked with his future boss. He got a call from the recruiter that same day who told Kevin that he was hired for a six-month contract, which had the possibility of turning into a full-time hire.

He was extremely excited. As it turned out, he couldn't start for a month because of paperwork, background checks and a drug screening so that left him plenty of time to spend with Linda. One thing about Linda, of many that Kevin did not like, was the fact that Linda wanted to see him all the time. She had plans to go to Florida for a vacation just for a few days, by herself. She tried to get Kevin to go, but he said since he was not working, he did not have the money.

Linda said it was no problem and that she would pay for everything, including airfare, but Kevin still said no, which surprised me a little.

After a few days, Linda flew back from Florida and stopped by our house to see Kevin before she went home. I was not there at the time, but when I got home, he said to look at all the stuff on the kitchen island. There must have been 10 t-shirts, hats, candy and a multitude of other souvenir stuff from Florida.

"Oh my gosh, Kevin, did Linda buy you all of this?" I asked.

"Yes, mom, and I felt really embarrassed that she did this. Every time we go somewhere, she pays. One time we went to Walmart, and Linda kept asking, 'So do you want this?' and proceeded to throw the stuff in the cart. I asked her how she can afford it, and she told me that she has 10 credit cards with various limits. She uses all of them, then pays off the balance when the bill comes in.

"Mom, she rents a house, and it is filled with stuff…junk everywhere that you can see. There is just a path between rooms. I keep wanting to organize it because it drives me crazy," Kevin explained.

Kevin stays at her house and watches movies with her until late and then falls asleep, most nights.

One day, he came home and said that he and Linda were going to Branson, MO, for a long weekend.

"Well, Kevin, that is a big commitment. Do you have money for this?" I asked.

"Well, we're just friends mom, and I have a little money, but Linda said that she will pay for everything."

"I see some very big red flags here, Kevin. Linda is in her mid-40s and has never been married. Plus, you say that at times, her personality gets on your nerves. Are you going to go away for the weekend with her, so far from home and be ok with it?" I questioned.

"Yes, Mom, I really want to go to Branson," Kevin stated. I had to look up, as he sounded like his 16-year-old self.

46.

Kevin was supposed to go to Branson from Thursday through Sunday, all expenses paid by Linda, because he still was not working yet.

Late Sunday morning, the front door opened and in walked Kevin with his suitcase.

"Hey, I really didn't expect you until much later. Anything wrong?" I asked.

"Well, I just could not take her personality any longer and I got on her nerves as well, because we both decided that the weekend to Branson was a mistake. We broke off whatever relationship we had. I start work this week, so it is for the best," Kevin said. Who is this adult and what has happened to Kevin?

I would never tell him, but I was happy it did not work out. He needed to be by himself for a while. After getting out of a 10-year marriage, Wendy was still texting him from time to time. She found a boyfriend online that gave her all the love and attention that Kevin never gave her, so she said. Then Kevin told me that the guy had already moved in with her, and Kevin seemed fine with it.

47.

Kevin had been working for Shriner's Hospital for six months. He absolutely loved it. The home life, though, not so much. I think he was really getting tired of our tiny guest room and was ready to find an apartment.

He went online and found a few that were in his price range and on his way to work. However, because he had such bad debt and had so many credit cards, and he had only been at his job for a short while, he was turned down over and over.

"I don't understand, I have a good job and I paid off all of my credit cards," he said, sounding frustrated.

"Well, Kev, it takes a while for your credit score to catch up from your past. Why don't you wait a few more months and try again?" I suggested.

His eyes got big, and he just shook his head. "It's not like I hate living with you guys, I just want to live by myself," he explained.

Kevin's stepsister, Sara, lived about 30 minutes farther from us in Union. She suggested that he look out there, as the rent is quite a bit cheaper. I did not think that this was a good idea. The town is a little "white trash," and I thought he could do better. Sara lived about two miles from their father, Steve, who lived with his wife and her two grown sons in a mobile home that was over 30 years old.

Well, Kevin started researching what was out there and found two places for rent. One was a one bedroom/one-bath house, and the other was a townhouse. I told him not to do anything until we saw the places together.

So, one night after Larry got home from work, we took a ride to Union to see the properties. First, the smaller house, in our opinion, was unlivable. We got out of the car and were met with weeds and tall grass. Kevin punched the code into the lockbox to get in.

Why this dump even had a lockbox was beyond me. As we walked through the door, we were all struck immediately by a horrible smell. Someone or something has died in the place. The kitchen window was broken, you couldn't get into the fridge because there was no handle, the carpet was so filthy, I really didn't want to walk on it even with my shoes on. Looking out the back window into the messy backyard was a broken-down aluminum shed. Any wind gust of 10 miles per hour would have crumbled it to nothing.

"Let's get out of here and go to see the townhouse," I suggested. However, we couldn't get in to see the townhouse because the person could not meet with Kevin until next Wednesday morning. In the meantime, she would run his credit check, but he would need to send her $150.00 to get it started.

We drove through the townhouse property. There were kids, toys and bikes everywhere. People were hanging around outside talking on their phones or just smoking.

"Kevin, this property looks terrible from the outside," I stated.

"Well, let's see if I get approved, then we can make an appointment to see it," he suggested.

The realtor called Kevin the very next day and said that he had been approved and the townhouse would be ready for him to move into in three days. I told Kevin that the timeframe was too short for us to get people to help, trucks to rent, etc. He relayed my comment to the lady, and she said she couldn't hold it. If someone else came along that wanted it, then she would give it to them.

Kevin was very disappointed with this and continued to search for an apartment. A month and a half later, the lady who owned the townhouse asked Kevin if he was still interested. He said that he was. By this time, it was mid-August and she wanted him to move in at the end of the month. She told Kevin to send her the 1st month's rent and security deposit to her, via Bitcoin. Once she got the $1,750.00, she would have the lease ready for him to sign, unbeknownst to me, or I would have stopped it. Bitcoin? Really?

So, Kevin sent her the $1,750.00. He told his boss that he would be late coming in on Wednesday morning, because he was going to meet this lady and sign the lease.

One hour before he was going to leave, the rental lady called him and said that she couldn't meet with him that day, but he could meet with her assistant, however, if he chose to do this—it would be an additional $100.00, or he could wait a week to meet with her.

I happened to be in the same room as Kevin when he got this text. After he explained everything to me, I kindly told him that this whole process did not sound right to me. He called the lady and told her that he wanted his money back. She said all right but needed his banking information, account and routing numbers. By this time, Kevin knew better than to give out his account information and told her he wanted his money back in the form of a cashier's check. She then said she would do this and hung up.

I looked at Kevin and said, "You will never see that hard-earned money again, lesson learned."

Kevin was very upset but got ready for work and was on his way, when about an hour later, the rental lady called Kevin back and said that to get him the cashier's check, she would need $150.00 additional money to be sent to her. Kevin told her that a cashier's check was less than $5.00 and again, wanted his money back. She hung up on him.

48.

Kevin went to a corner bar not far from our house that he liked to frequent. On Wednesday nights, he was on a trivia team. One of his team members was a girl named Tammy. Kevin and Tammy get along well. She rented a small house in Pacific which was just one town past our house.

"How was trivia last night?" I inquired one Thursday.

"It was fine, we came in third place. Tammy wasn't there again. They said that she had to quit her job and move home to Springfield to take care of her dad," Kevin said.

"Oh, my goodness, I hope he will be okay," I said.

Later that day, Kevin called and said that he'd heard from Tammy. She wanted to know if he was still looking for a place to rent. She said her landlord was putting her small house on the market and asked him if he was still interested. Kevin said, "Sure."

The landlord called Kevin that afternoon. They talked for quite a while. He knew about Kevin being scammed and felt sorry for him. He said that Kevin could have the house if he wanted it, based on the great recommendation that Tammy gave to him. He also said that since Kevin had gotten scammed, he would give him one month to save up for the rent and security deposit and hold the house for him.

Since Kevin already knew what the house looked like, he didn't need to see it. He was over the moon excited and couldn't wait to move in. Once he told everyone he was going to move, he started packing and planning.

I, on the other hand, was a little less excited. He hadn't lived on his own since meeting Wendy when he was just coming off drug rehab. So, running through my mind was —is he going to go back to drugs, or is he going to renew his interest in online dating scams for money? I mentioned these fears to Kevin, but he empathically said 'no' to both.

Brian and his fiancé were getting married in Dallas and Kevin was going to be included in the wedding. He was so excited to be doing this. Kevin loved his brother so very much that although he wasn't the best man, he wanted to write a speech for him.

Brother meaning —trust, bond, love, friendship, unity, strength, togetherness.

What can I say about my brother that some of you don't know? Well, here goes,

My brother is the best brother another bro could have. He would give the shirt off his back to anyone and help anyone in need. I wasn't close to my brother growing up, meaning that we never hung out as normal brothers should. As you may know, I was sick most of my childhood, but he was always there and some of the time I didn't even know it. It wasn't till my bro went off to college that I realized I needed him more than ever. That day was sad for me watching him leave the house and I couldn't go with him to see him leave. I realized that I was about to start my own journey and he was about to start his own too. I am so proud of what my bro has accomplished in his life and appreciate everything he has done for me. I missed my bro for so many years but now I have my bro back. He is himself and true to his nature since meeting Jeanine. I haven't seen my bro so happy in a long time and I have Jeanine to thank for that. I am so proud of what you have done with your life and your accomplishments. I don't have the words to explain the love that I have for you, but you are the best brother in the world, and I wouldn't change it for all the money in the world. Now on to Jeanine. I wanted to tell you that you are the best sister-in-law in the world. Ever since we met you have cared for me like you have known me your entire life. You make my brother so happy, and I consider you like a sister I never had. I love you both very much and I want to officially welcome you to our family as if you weren't already lol. I wish you both to have the best life together for many years to come.

Love, your brother Kevin

PS: You're not a real doctor, you're my brother.

49.

Moving day came in a hurry. Larry's brother's company was closing, and the owner was moving back to Colorado. He gave all his furniture, dishes, pots and pans, etc., to Kevin. Suddenly, everyone had certain things that they were willing to part with to make his house a home.

Our house felt empty without Kevin living here. I would stay awake waiting for him to come home. The dogs kept walking into the guest room and slowly returned to the kitchen.

One Saturday morning, I opened my computer to find an email from Kevin. As I was reading it, the tears just kept rolling down my face. He had emailed me the lyrics to "Don't Stop Believing" by Journey.

Kevin's journey is far from being over.

What's next?

Casey Clark has had her own marketing firm for over 20 years. She was awarded the Businessperson of the Year in 1999. She has been published in many trade newspapers and magazines. This is Ms. Clark's second novel. She lives just outside of St. Louis, MO with her husband, Larry, and two spoiled basset hounds.

Acknowledgments

Thank you to everyone who continually supports me in my writing career. Thanks to Jessie Saltzman for editing this book. Also, my Sassy Seven girls who always believed in me. My best friend Julie, for over 50 years. I could not have made it this far without you by my side. My husband Larry, whose love and support is unconditional. And to my oldest son, Brian, who is always there when I need him.